AN INSTANT GUIDE TO

INSECTS

The most familiar species of
North American insects
described and illustrated in color

Pamela Forey and Cecilia Fitzsimons

BONANZA BOOKS
New York

First published 1987 by Bonanza Books,
distributed by Crown Publishers, Inc.

© 1987 Atlantis Publications Ltd.

Printed in Spain by Sirven Grafic

D.L. B.1928-1990

ISBN: 0-517-63547-X

Contents

INTRODUCTION   8

HOW TO USE THIS BOOK   8

GUIDE TO IDENTIFICATION   8

LIFE HISTORY OF INSECTS   12

BEETLES   14

BUTTERFLIES & MOTHS   40

FLIES   57

BEES, WASPS & ANTS   76

BUGS   90

HOMOPTERAN BUGS   99

GRASSHOPPERS, KATYDIDS & CRICKETS   105

OTHER INSECTS   109

INDEX   122

Introduction

There are about 90,000 species of insects in North America. They are a huge group of animals, by far the largest single group in the continent and in the whole world. They are enormously important in the impact that they have on the environment; they pollinate the flowers of many native plants and trees as well as crops and fruits, so that without them those crops would not set seed; others we class as pests since they eat the leaves, fruits and roots of native plants, crops and trees, causing great destruction and high economic losses; more subtly, many others act as regulators of the pests, since they prey on them, parasitize them and keep their populations under control; yet others carry diseases like malaria and typhoid. A world without insects is unimaginable; they occupy crucial positions in every habitat in the land and play key roles in supporting and maintaining the present balance of nature.

Whole libraries are devoted solely to insects and a book of this size cannot provide anything but an introduction to them, a hint of their diversity and form. However it will enable the reader to identify many of the major insect families and to allocate many insects to their proper place within the group as a whole. Thus, with this book, the reader will be able first to identify an insect as a beetle, for example, and then to decide that it is a tiger beetle, belonging to the tiger beetle family.

How to use this book

We have divided the book into sections based mainly on the biology of the insects themselves; however we have grouped the many smaller groups of insects like springtails, mayflies, lacewings, etc. together in a section at the end, even though they are unrelated to each other. The sections are **Beetles; Butterflies and Moths; Flies; Bees, Wasps and Ants; Bugs; Homopteran Bugs; Grasshoppers, Katydids and Crickets; Other Insects**. If you are confident that you can identify an insect, as a beetle or butterfly for example, you will be able to turn directly to the section on beetles or butterflies to identify it more accurately. If however, you are unsure of the major group to which it belongs then you can use the key in the *Guide to Identification* which follows on the next page, to find the right section.

Guide to identification

Insects are distinguished from all other animals by the following features: they have bodies with hard exoskeletons, divided into three sections (head, thorax and abdomen); there are two antennae on the head; and three pairs of legs and two pairs of wings on the thorax.

In this guide we have used the differences in the wings of the various groups of insects to enable you to identify the group to which any insect belongs. Page numbers given at the end of each category will enable you to turn directly to the relevant section.

Wingless Insects. Very primitive insects, together with some others, never have wings at any time of their lives. These include the primitive Springtails and Silverfish (*120, 121*) and the Fleas and Lice (*119*). Other insects have wingless forms as well as winged individuals; these include the Ants (*89*) and Termites (*111*) which both have wingless workers in the nest; Walkingsticks (*118*) are usually wingless; many species of Earwigs (*110*) are wingless; females of Oriental Cockroaches (*109*) are wingless as are females of some species of Fireflies (*24*).

Insects in which the fore wings are different to the hind wings. In several groups of insects the fore wings are hardened and strengthened while the hind wings, which are the wings used for flight, are membranous. When the insect is on the ground or at rest, the delicate hind wings are covered and protected by the fore wings. In Grasshoppers (*105–108*) and Cockroaches (*109*) the fore wings are long and narrow, and although they are thickened and leathery they still retain veins. Their hind wings are folded like fans under the fore wings when not in use. Earwigs (*110*) have very short leathery fore wings and the membranous hind wings are folded like fans beneath them. Mantises (*118*) also have long, narrow, thickened fore wings. In Bugs (*90–98*) the base of each fore wing is leathery and often colored while the tip is membranous. In Beetles (*14–39*) the fore wings are veinless, very tough or even hard, and they meet in a straight line down the center of the back.

Insects which have two pairs of membranous wings. Several groups of insects have two similar pairs of membranous wings. These include the Homopteran Bugs (*99–104*), Termites, Mayflies, Stoneflies, Dragonflies and Damselflies (*111–115*), and Lacewings (*117*). Caddisflies (*116*) also have two pairs of membranous wings but they differ from the others in being hairy and may look like moths. Bees, wasps and ants (*76–89*) often look as if they have only one pair of wings, even though they actually have two pairs. This is because the leading edge of the smaller hind wing is hooked on to the trailing edge of the fore wing.

Insects which have two pairs of scale-covered wings. Butterflies and moths (*40–56*) are immediately distinguished from other insects by their large, often multi-colored, scale-covered wings. Caddisflies (*116*) are rather similar to moths, but with hairy, rather than scale-covered, wings.

Insects which have only one pair of wings. In the Flies (*57–75*) only the fore wings are developed as wings. The hind wings are modified into small knobs which act as balancing organs — they can be seen quite clearly just behind the fore wings. Bees, ants and wasps (*76–89*) may be confused with flies for they often look as if they have only one pair of wings; however careful examination will reveal that they have two pairs of wings hooked together and they do not have balancing organs.

Making a positive identification

Once you have decided to which group your insect belongs, turn to the relevant section. At the beginning of the first seven sections, you will find a page which gives you detailed distinguishing features of the group together with illustrations of four representative species.

Following this there will be a page for each major family, with other composite pages where smaller families are featured. On pages where major families are described you will find the name of the family at the top of the page, together with two other pieces of information: the number of species in the family and the length of the insect (wingspan is given instead of length in butterflies and moths). Size symbols also provide a quick guide to the insect's size.

Fig. 1 Key to size symbols

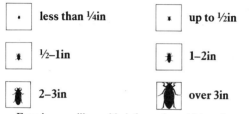

	less than ¼in		up to ½in
	½–1in		1–2in
	2–3in		over 3in

Four boxes will provide information which makes positive identification possible. Throughout the text, numbers indicate the name(s) of the insects illustrated on the page. The first box provides details of features or combinations of features which are characteristic of that insect family.

The second box gives you information about the biology of the adults, where they are likely to be found and what they feed on. If they bite, sting or cause skin irritation, a warning sign has been included in the illustration.

Fig. 2 Warning.

These insects may bite, sting or cause skin irritation

The third box provides a description of the larvae, whether they are pests, where they are likely to be found and what they feed on. A numbered illustration of the larva is included on many pages.

The fourth box provides some idea of variation in the family and gives details of the illustrations on the page. Names printed in heavy type are of insects illustrated in the book, those printed in ordinary type are not.

Illustrations are of one or more common species from the family, and include a distribution map which provides at a glance information about the distribution of these insects in N. America.

Fig. 3 Distribution map

● Members of this family are widespread or common in this area.

○ Some species from this family are found in this area.

Other Common Families

In many places throughout the book, you will find pages of smaller or less common insect families, where up to four families are featured together on one page. A brief description of each is given, together with some details of the biology of the animals.

Fig. 4 Specimen Page

Color of band denotes group of insects

Length

Name of insect family

BLISTER BEETLES
up to 1in   about 300 species

Size symbol

Number of species in family

Bites or stings!

Larva

Color illustration of common species

Distribution map

♂ Male

♀ Female

Elongated, soft-bodied or leathery beetles with a broad head and narrow neck. Usually black or brown, with long legs and thread-like antennae. Some have bright red or yellow markings. Fore wings cover body loosely and are sometimes shortened.

Characteristics of adult

Adults can be pests in gardens, on potatoes, tomatoes or other crops, also on apples. Their blood contains cantharidin, a dangerous poison which also irritates the skin.

Biology of adult

Larvae (1) are parasites on egg-cases of grasshoppers or in bees' nests. First stage larvae are long-legged and active and cling to legs of host to be carried to the bees' nest or grasshoppers' eggs. Later stages are grub-like and inactive.

Characteristics & biology of larva

Striped Blister Beetles (2) are garden pests on potatoes and tomatoes but larvae control grasshopper numbers. Oil beetles (3), mostly found in late fall or early spring, give off an unpleasant oily fluid when disturbed. The European species, Spanish Fly, is used as a source of commercial cantharidin.

Common & illustrated species

21

Life history of insects

Basically insects have two different kinds of life history. Primitive insects, including grasshoppers, bugs, mayflies and dragonflies lay eggs which hatch into nymphs, small wingless editions of the adults which usually lead a similar life to the adults and which gradually develop wings as they grow and molt. The wings are fully formed and the insects are mature after the nymph undergoes the final molt.

By contrast more advanced insects, including bees, wasps, flies, butterflies, moths and beetles have a two-phase life cycle in which the larvae or young stages are quite different in appearance and habits to adults. They grow with each molt but never have wing buds. At the penultimate molt they change into a pupa or chrysalis in which dramatic changes take place, and the larva metamorphoses into an adult. At the final molt the pupa breaks open and the adult emerges.

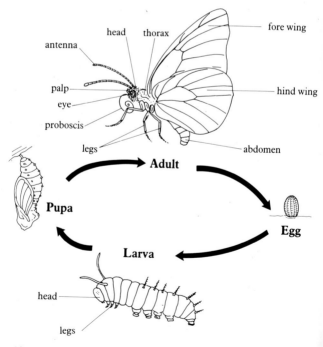

Illustrated glossary of terms

Bee-bread   A mixture of nectar and pollen.

Honeydew   A sugary liquid produced by some insects.

Molt   Because of their hard skin (or exoskeleton), insects cannot grow continuously like many other animals; instead they molt (shed their skin) periodically throughout their lives and grow rapidly while the new skin is still soft, before the new skin hardens.

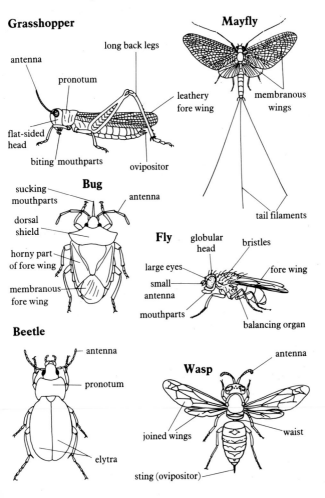

Grasshopper

long back legs

antenna

pronotum

leathery
fore wing

flat-sided
head

biting mouthparts

ovipositor

Mayfly

membranous
wings

tail filaments

Bug

sucking
mouthparts

antenna

dorsal
shield

horny part
of fore wing

membranous
fore wing

Fly   globular
head

bristles

large eyes

fore wing

small
antenna

mouthparts

balancing organ

Beetle

antenna

pronotum

elytra

Wasp

antenna

joined wings

waist

sting (ovipositor)

13

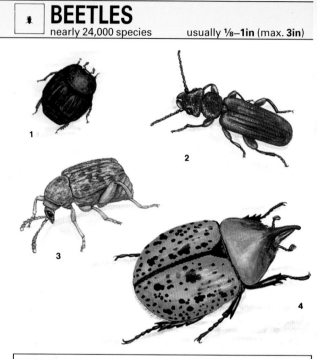

Distinctive insects with horny or leathery fore wings called elytra which meet in a straight line in the center of the back.
Membranous flying wings are folded under elytra when insect is at rest. Antennae usually have 11 segments.

Beetles may be aquatic, some live in wood, others in fungi or on flowers and leaves; some are household pests. Many adults feed on plants, others are hunters, catching insects.

Larva has well-developed hard head, a thorax and a soft or hard abdomen. Active predaceous forms have well-developed legs and antennae, soil and wood-boring forms are often legless and grub-like with soft bodies.

Largest order of animals with 300,000 species in the world. They vary in size from the tiny minute beetles (less than 1/16in long) to the giant Hercules beetles (1½–2⅜in). Illustrated on this page are **Clown Beetle (1)**; **Red Flat Bark Beetle (2)**; **Bean Weevil (3)**; and **Eastern Hercules Beetle (4)**.

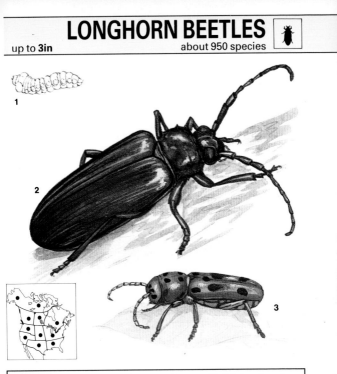

Elongated, cylindrical beetles, many large and brightly colored. Distinctive antennae at least half as long as body and often much longer, up to three times body length. The base of the antenna is often partially surrounded by the eye.

Many can be seen by day feeding on flower nectar or pollen. They move and fly swiftly, remaining still if disturbed or squeaking if picked up. Others are nocturnal, hiding by day.

Larvae (**1**) are round-headed borers, pale and elongated with reduced legs, brown heads and powerful jaws; they bore into wood, making a hole in the bark with sawdust around. Many are pests in forests and orchards but most live in rotting wood.

A large family of distinctive beetles. Pests, like the **Great Pine Borer** (**2**), bore into conifers, cottonwoods and citrus. Larvae of twig pruners tunnel in twigs, making them fall off. Raspberry Cane Borers are pests in raspberries and blackberries. **Milkweed beetles** (**3**) are often seen on milkweeds.

15

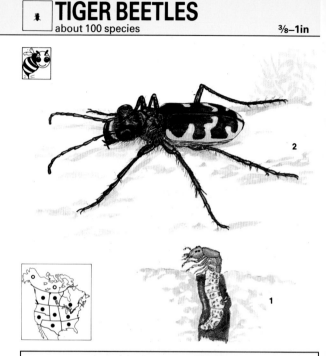

Fast-moving beetles with elongated cylindrical bodies and long legs. Many are metallic green or brown with lighter patterns; others are black or dull in color. Head and eyes are large, head wider than pronotum; antennae thread-like.

Active by day. Found on paths, in woods and on sandy shores. Active hunters and difficult to catch, with fast movements and sudden flight. They may bite if handled incautiously.

Larvae (1) long, whitish grubs with large heads and powerful jaws. They live in vertical burrows in hard ground, waiting at top of burrow for prey to venture close and then seizing them. Smooth circular depression surrounds mouth of burrow.

Common tiger beetles, like the **Beautiful Tiger Beetle** (2), may be green or bronze with various patterns; most are found in the west but Beautiful Tiger Beetles are found throughout N. America. Dejean's Tiger Beetle is a black species which cannot fly; it lives west of the Rockies.

16

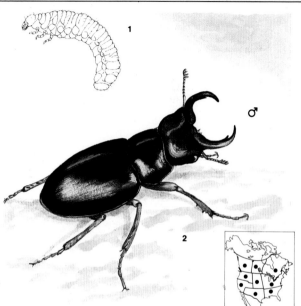

1

♂

2

Moderately large to large, flattened, heavy, brown or black beetles. Antennae elbowed with clubs consisting of three or four plates. Males have large, sometimes antler-like jaws; those of female similar but smaller.

Nocturnal. Found in woods, on sandy beaches, in towns where they hide by day beneath logs and stumps. Adults feed on sap or may not feed at all. They may be attracted to lights.

Eggs laid in crevices of bark. Larvae (1) are curled into a C-shape, and live in decaying wood of stumps and logs, feeding on the juices formed by the decaying wood.

Red-Brown Stag Beetles (2) live in deciduous woods and in cities in eastern USA, near maples, apples and other trees. American Stag Beetles are found in eastern USA in oak stumps. Others are associated with trees like cottonwood, aspen, birch, cedar, oaks throughout N. America.

17

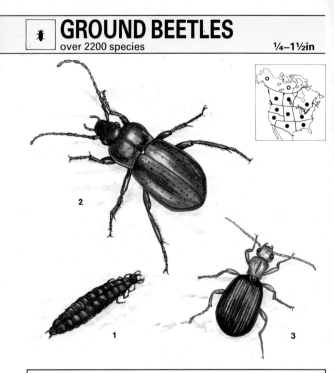

Elongated, rather flattened beetles with long legs which have spurs. Mostly black in color but some are brightly colored. Pronotum often narrower than elytra and head narrower than pronotum. Antennae thread-like.

Nocturnal. Adults rarely fly but can run fast. Hide by day under stones, debris or logs. Hunt prey by night, including pests like cutworms, gypsy moth caterpillars and slugs.

Larvae (1) have long flattened bodies, well-developed legs and sharp jaws. They live in underground burrows or hide in similar places to adults, but are less likely to venture out. They are active predators like adults.

Snail eaters are common large black or brown beetles. They often have purple edges to the elytra, as does the **European Ground Beetle** (2). Black ground beetles are common throughout the continent. **Bombardier beetles** (3) spray toxic liquid from anal glands as a defense mechanism.

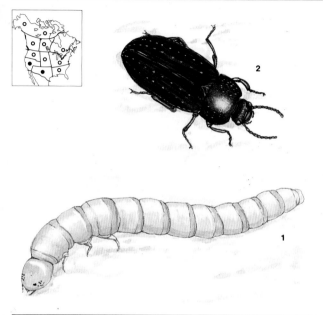

Hard-bodied, oval or oblong beetles, often awkward and slow-moving. Most are black, some with white or red markings; many have striated or roughened elytra. Antennae are thread-like or bead-like; their origin on the head cannot be seen from above.

Usually nocturnal. Mostly western desert beetles which remain on the ground, hiding by day under bark, plant debris or dung. Some are crop pests. Some attack dried foods and clothes.

Larvae are scavengers like adults, living in similar places and feeding on similar foods. Many are shiny and cylindrical in form (false wireworms). Mealworms (1) are pests in stored grains and are used as food for pet amphibians and reptiles.

Eleodes beetles (2) may occur in huge numbers in spring and summer in southwest; their false wireworm larvae feed on newly planted seeds of wheat and corn. Ironclad and Forked Fungus Beetles are western woodland species with hard, warty elytra. Mealworm and Flour Beetles are grain and flour pests.

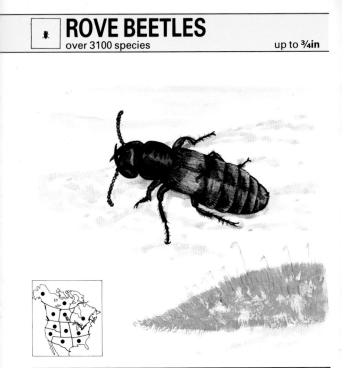

Slender, elongated, parallel-sided beetles with short elytra which leave most of the abdomen exposed. Abdomen flexible, often bent upwards, especially when disturbed. Usually dull-colored, often black. Antennae thread-like or clubbed.

Found on carrion or fungi, decaying plant material or under stones, logs or debris, in wet places and in flowers. Most are active predators on other insects, can run fast and fly well.

Larvae similar to adults but wingless. They are predators like the adults and are found in similar places.

Large rove beetles (including the **Gray and Black Rove Beetle** illustrated) are found in dung, carcasses, fungi and rotting vegetation. The little Obscure rove beetles live in similar places. Spiny-legged rove beetles mostly live in wet places and mud; many of them make burrows in the mud.

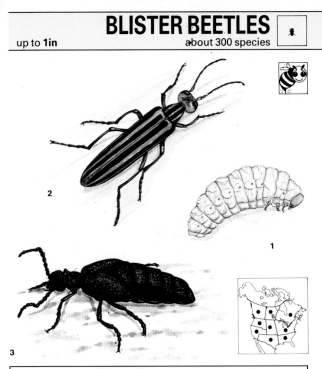

Elongated, soft-bodied or leathery beetles with a broad head and narrow neck. Usually black or brown, with long legs and thread-like antennae. Some have bright red or yellow markings. Fore wings cover body loosely and are sometimes shortened.

Adults can be pests in gardens, on potatoes, tomatoes or other crops, also on apples. Their blood contains cantharidin, a dangerous poison which also irritates the skin.

Larvae (1) are parasites on egg-cases of grasshoppers or in bees' nests. First stage larvae are long-legged and active and cling to legs of host to be carried to the bees' nest or grasshoppers' eggs. Later stages are grub-like and inactive.

Striped Blister Beetles (2) are garden pests on potatoes and tomatoes but larvae control grasshopper numbers. **Oil beetles** (3), mostly found in late fall or early spring, give off an unpleasant oily fluid when disturbed. The European species, Spanish Fly, is used as a source of commercial cantharidin.

21

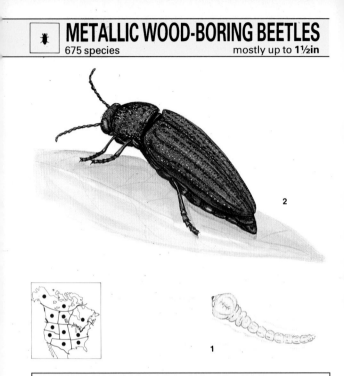

Hard-bodied, elongated, parallel-sided, rather flattened beetles. Elytra and underside often metallic red, green or blue in color; surface of elytra usually grooved or pitted. Elytra do not move in flight. Antennae short and thread-like.

Active by day and bask in sunshine on trees in woods or orchards. Feed on leaves of trees and plants. If disturbed they drop to ground and feign death or fly away.

Larvae (1) are called flat-headed borers and have an enlarged, flattened thorax. Bore into trunks and roots of trees, also into stumps and cut timber and usually make a gallery just below the bark. Others are leaf-miners. Some produce galls.

Many are pests, like the Flat-headed Apple Borers which infest apple, pear, elm, maple, oak and other trees throughout the continent. Others attack chestnut, hickory, aspen, birch, cedar, pine, hemlock etc. The **Golden Buprestid (2)** is a western species whose larvae attack conifers.

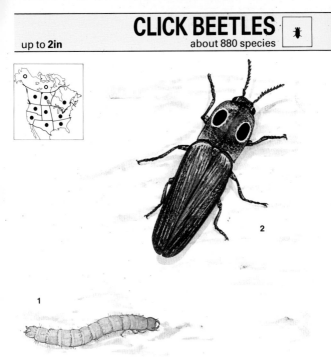

Distinctive beetles because of the way they can flip into the air if they fall on their backs. They turn over several times in the air and may land right way up; if not they flip again. They are flattened and elongated, usually brown or black.

Adults live on leaves and flowers of herbaceous plants, in decaying wood or under bark. Many do not feed at all while others feed on leaves.

Larvae are wireworms (**1**); hard-bodied, shiny, brown or yellow in color, cylindrical in shape. Most live in soil, feeding on seeds or roots. Many are pests in fields of grains and other crops. Others are predators in decaying wood or under bark.

Lantern click beetles are nocturnal species which live in decaying wood; they glow in flight. **Eyed Elators** (**2**) live in mixed woods east of the Rockies. Many wireworms are pests, like the Potato and Tomato Wireworms of southeastern USA and the Prairie Grain Wireworm of the central states.

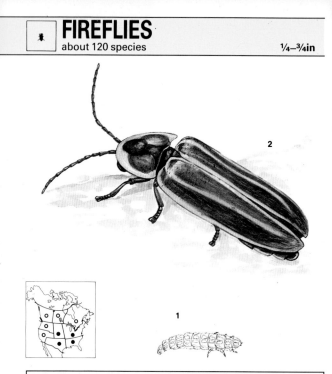

2

1

Soft-bodied, elongated beetles with rather soft elytra, dull brown, olive or black in color. Pronotum expanded forwards to cover head. Antennae thread-like. Light organs on the underside of the abdomen produce flashes of yellow or green light.

Appear at twilight on summer nights usually in woods, but also in meadows or beside water. Males fly but some females are wingless. Males flash in flight, females from the ground.

Larvae (**1**) and wingless females are called glow-worms. Larvae are also luminous, living in debris on woodland floor, in wet places or under bark, where they prey on insects and other invertebrates.

Fireflies are the only insects which flash light, other insects which produce light glow continuously. Light flash pattern and color are unique to each species, for instance **Pennsylvania Fireflies** (**2**) flash green. Eastern and woods fireflies include several common species east of the Rockies.

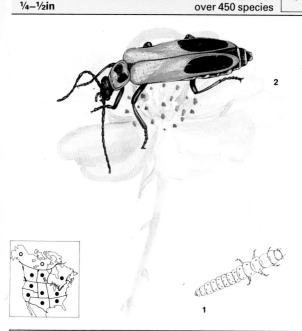

1

2

Elongated, more or less parallel-sided, soft-bodied beetles with leathery elytra, like slender fireflies but they do not produce light. Usually brown or black, but may be yellow or red. The pronotum is not extended over the head.

Found on flowers and leaves of a variety of plants, like milkweeds and goldenrods or shrubs like hydrangeas and blackberries. Feed on pollen or catch other insects like aphids.

Larvae (1) appear velvety, with a dense covering of hairs and are often dark in color. They are usually predaceous, living in soil, beneath bark and in debris and catching soft-bodied insects, like caterpillars or fly maggots.

Pennsylvania Leatherwings (2) are found in meadows and gardens east of the Rockies. Downy Soldier Beetles are common in fields and gardens, or on giant ragweed where they feed on aphids. Goldenrod Soldier Beetles, from eastern USA, feed on pollen; their larvae prey on other insect larvae.

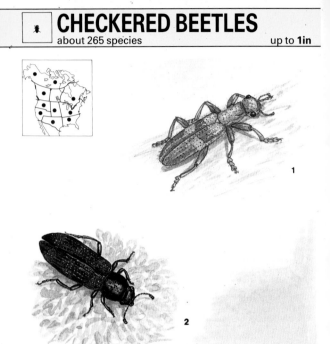

CHECKERED BEETLES

about 265 species

up to **1in**

Small, brightly colored, patterned or checkered beetles with hairy, elongated bodies and rather soft elytra. They have large heads and clubbed antennae.

Most common in woodland, on flowers and trees, usually on or under the bark or on the flowers, not on the leaves. Feed on pollen or on the larvae and adults of bark-boring beetles.

Many larvae live in the galleries of bark beetles, where they hunt for the larvae of the bark beetles. Others attack the larvae of gall-forming beetles or of bees and wasps. Some feed on moth caterpillars. A few feed on stored meats.

Many are important predators in woodland areas where species like the **Slender Checkered Beetles** (**1**) feed on destructive beetles. **Ornate Checkered Beetles** (**2**) feed on wasp and bee larvae. Ham Beetles are scavengers and feed on carrion and blowfly larvae; they may also be pests on smoked meats.

BARK & AMBROSIA BEETLES

up to ½in   about 480 species

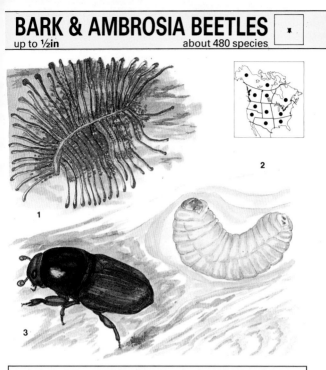

1

2

3

Elongated, cylindrical, brown or black beetles with pitted or striated elytra. Antennae short and elbowed, usually with a large rounded club. The elaborate tunnels cut by the adults into wood have distinctive patterns (**1**), depending on species.

Bark Beetles attack dead or dying trees, making elaborate tunnels just below bark. Ambrosia Beetles tunnel into heartwood; tunnels lined with fungus (ambrosia) on which they feed.

Larvae (**2**) are small, whitish, legless and curled into a C-shape. They are found in tunnels usually cut at right angles to the main tunnels of the adults. They feed in same way as the adults.

Ambrosia beetles attack hardwood and coniferous trees of many kinds, usually through an injury. They cause serious damage or death of the tree and their pinhole borings ruin the lumbar value of the wood. The adults (**3**) of **European Elm Bark Beetle**, which is illustrated, carry Dutch Elm Disease.

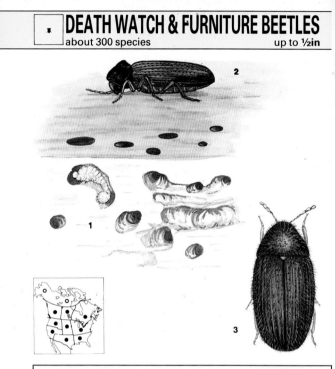

Dark brown to black beetles, often elongated and cylindrical but may be oval. Their legs can be pressed closely against the body. Pronotum expanded forwards to form hood-like cover over head. Last three segments of antennae lengthened and expanded.

Adults are most likely to be found in old woodland with a lot of dead wood. They are often overlooked for they feign death when disturbed, drawing in their legs and keeping still.

Larvae (1) make burrows in wood of buildings and furniture, or in dead wood of trees, leaving fine wood powder beneath wood. They can make wood unsafe and reduce it to powder form, given time. Adults emerge through small holes.

Furniture Beetles (2) and death watch beetles may infest furniture or structural timbers in old buildings. Death watch beetles make a tapping sound as a mating call, supposedly a portent of death. Related **Drugstore** (3) and Tobacco Beetles live with their larvae in dried vegetables, spices or tobacco.

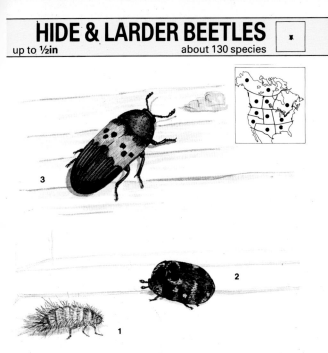

Small, elongated, brown or black beetles, often covered in pale gray scales or hairs that can easily be rubbed off. They look as if they have pale gray markings. They may feign death if disturbed. Antennae short and clubbed.

Adults are scavengers on hide and hair of carrion. Also pests in houses, feeding on stored foods, wool, fur, feathers, meat, cheese etc. Some are museum pests, damaging stuffed specimens.

Larvae are active, hairy and grub-like; some, clothed in long brown hairs, are called buffalo bugs (1). Most are similar in habits to the adults and can do considerable damage.

Carpet Beetles (2) may be found on flowers or in windows; their buffalo bug larvae (1) are destructive to carpets, fabrics and museum collections. **Larder Beetles** (3) feed on carrion in the wild but are pests in the home, eating meat and cheese. Hide Beetles are used in museums to clean bones.

29

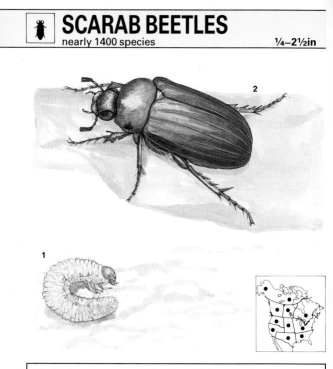

Mostly short, stout, convex beetles, with large heads. The distinctive antennae are elbowed, with clubs formed of 7–11 leaf-like segments. The beetles vary in color from dull brown to metallic green or blue and some have bright markings.

Adults mostly feed on leaves, pollen, sap or fruits and are found on plants; some are pests on crops. Others feed on fungi or rotting vegetation.

Larvae (1) are usually C-shaped with white bodies and brown heads. They live in a variety of habitats; many live in the soil and damage lawns and crops by feeding on roots, others live in dung, carrion, under bark and in rotting vegetation.

A diverse family, including chafers, **May beetles** (2) and June bugs; **tumblebugs** and **dung beetles**; rain beetles; Rhinoceros and **Hercules beetles**; flower beetles; and the **Japanese Beetle**. Chafers, May beetles and June bugs may fly to lights at night; their larvae live in the soil and feed on plant roots.

SCARAB BEETLES

Dung Beetles and Tumblebugs
Mostly black, some bronze or
green & some males have horns.
Found in or near carrion & dung
on which they feed.
Tumblebugs (1) roll a ball of
dung away, inserting an egg into
it & burying the ball. Larvae
develop inside. Dung Beetles lay
eggs in dung or in holes beneath
it.

Japanese Beetle (2)
Deep green, shining beetle with
metallic brown elytra,
introduced from Asia. Serious
pest in eastern USA, adults feed
on leaves of many plants &
larvae eat roots.

Flower Beetles
Mostly small, flattened beetles in
which elytra do not cover the
sides of the abdomen. Adults
mostly found on flowers where
they feed on pollen & nectar.
Their elytra do not open in flight
& they make a loud buzzing
sound when flying. **Green June
Beetle (3)** is a large robust
beetle, found on flowers & fruits
of many plants & trees in eastern
& southern states, especially in
sandy areas. **Bumble Flower
Beetle (4)**, from eastern USA,
feeds on fruit as well as pollen.

31

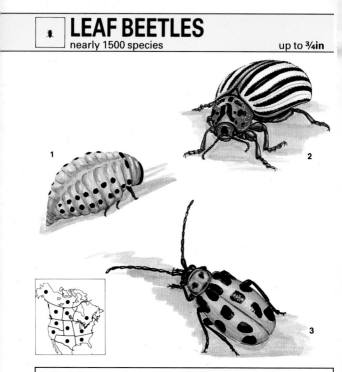

Small, oval and convex in outline. These beetles are often metallic in appearance and attractively marked with various colors. Antennae short, less than half the length of the body, thread-like, clubbed or saw-toothed. Eyes not notched.

Found on all kinds of native plants, crops and trees, often together with their larvae. They feed on leaves, pollen and flowers.

Larvae (1) feed on roots or leaves. Many are serious pests, biting holes in leaves to defoliate plants or trees if present in high numbers. Others are tiny and mine tunnels in leaves; tunnels appear as pale lines meandering across the leaf.

A large family and probably the most damaging beetle family in N. America. Included in it are **flea beetles**, **case-bearing leaf beetles** and **tortoise beetles**, as well as many leaf beetles and leaf-miners, like the **Colorado Potato Beetle** (2), **Spotted Cucumber Beetle** (3), and Asparagus Beetle.

Case-bearing Beetles (2)
Small cylindrical beetles with long antennae. Head almost "buried" in thorax. Found on many native plants & trees like willow, birch & oak. Larvae may camouflage themselves with excrement.

Tortoise Beetles (3)
Almost circular, flattened beetles with elytra expanded to cover body & head, like a small turtle. Larvae oval, flattened & spiny & attach cast skin to forked "tail." Adults & larvae bite small holes in plants like morning glories, milkweeds, tomatoes.

Flea Beetles (1)
Small bluish or black beetles with large hind legs adapted for jumping. Adults feed on leaves, producing tiny holes like shot; larvae feed on roots. Many are important pests which, in large numbers, may defoliate the plants they feed on. There are grapevine, tomato, sweet potato & corn flea beetles amongst many others. They also cause damage to a variety of native plants, like willows, sumac, dock & clovers.

33

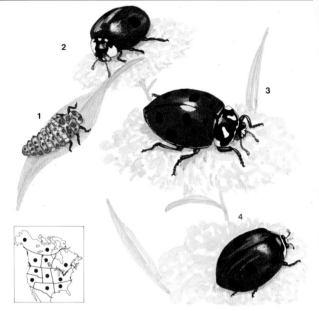
Round or broadly oval and hemispherical in outline, brightly colored red and yellow or black and brown, usually with black, white, red or yellow spots. Pronotum partly or completely covers the head. Antennae end in three-segmented clubs.

Predators, feeding on aphids, thrips, scale insects, mites and other pests, found on plants wherever their prey are present. They may sometimes be found overwintering in large groups.

Larvae (1) are variable in form, often camouflaged and spiky, dark in color or pale and wax-covered. They are voracious predators like the adults, feeding on the same insect pests. Eggs are laid by a female near a colony of the prey species.

The familiar red ladybirds have up to 15 spots; they include the **2-spot** (2), **Convergent** (3) and **9-spot** (4) **Ladybirds**. Black ladybirds may have up to ten yellow or reddish spots; others have stripes. Unusual members of the family are the Mexican Bean Beetle and Squash Ladybird, both destructive species.

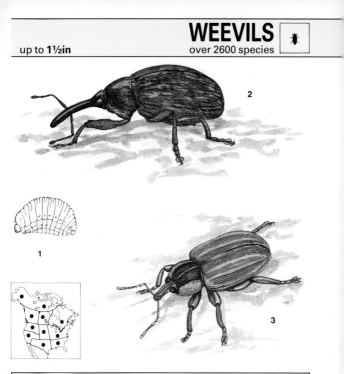

Distinctive, hard-bodied beetles with long snouts and elbowed antennae. These antennae arise part way along the snout.

Found on plants. Adults chew holes in the leaves and may cause extensive damage. They often feign death if disturbed and fall to the ground.

Eggs laid in soil or inside nuts, fruits or stems by female who bores a hole with her long snout. Larvae (**1**) short, whitish and curled, with small dark heads and no legs. Feed on roots, nuts or fruit and often do more damage than adults.

Most weevils are pests whose larvae cause great damage to plants. The **Cotton Boll Weevil** (**2**), Rose Weevil, pine weevils and chestnut weevils are amongst the most notorious. Others attack cabbages, grapes, strawberries and corn. Several weevils, like **Lesser Clover Weevil** (**3**), feed on clovers.

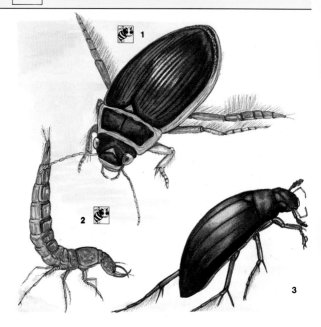

Predaceous Diving Beetles (1)
475 species. Streamlined, shiny,
black or brownish beetles with
yellow markings, ¼–1in long.
Hind legs flattened & fringed
with long hairs; they are moved
together in swimming. Antennae
thread-like. These are predators,
living in ponds & streams
throughout N. America, &
hunting insects, tadpoles &
small fishes. Often seen head
down at water surface, with
abdomen projecting into the air,
absorbing air. Larvae (2) are
"water tigers," attacking prey
larger than themselves.

Water Scavenger Beetles (3)
About 280 species. Black, oval,
streamlined beetles, up to 1½in
long. Antennae short, with
terminal clubs. Hind legs
flattened & fringed with hairs,
moved alternately in swimming.
They live in ponds & still waters,
throughout N. America. They
hang, head up, at the water
surface & pull air down over
their underside to form a silver
bubble, which they take down
with them. Scavengers on plant
& animal remains; larvae are
large & voracious hunters,
feeding on aquatic animals.

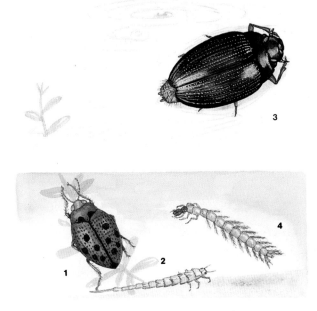

Crawling Water Beetles (1)
70 species. Small, oval beetles, up to ½in long, pointed at both ends, yellow or brown in color with black spots. Found in much of N. America, in ponds, lakes & streams where they crawl slowly on the bottom. They feed on the vegetation and on any insects that they can catch. Larvae (2) are slender & their body segments have fleshy lobes with spiny tips. They live in similar habitats to the adults & feed on plants, especially on filamentous algae.

Whirligig Beetles (3)
About 60 species. Black, oval, streamlined beetles, ¼–¾in long, with short antennae. Middle & hind legs flattened & paddle-like, front legs long & slender. Found throughout N. America; they swim on ponds, resting on the water surface or on plants & swimming in rapid zigzags if disturbed. Their eyes are divided horizontally for seeing in air & water. They feed on insects trapped in water. Larvae (4) slender & whitish with gills on sides of abdomen; hunt on bottom for insect larvae.

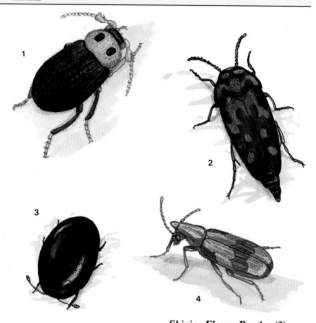

Soft-winged Flower Beetles (1)
520 species. Soft-bodied, egg-shaped beetles, up to ½in long, with soft elytra and saw-toothed antennae. Black, blue or green, often with bright markings. Adults feed on pollen, other insects or insect eggs.

Tumbling Flower Beetles (2)
About 200 species. Wedge-shaped beetles with arched backs, normally black or gray with colored scales. Adults associated especially with members of the carrot family. When threatened they jump & tumble to the ground.

Shining Flower Beetles (3)
About 120 species. Small convex, shining beetles, about ¼in long, brown or black in color. Both adults & larvae are found on flowers like goldenrods, sunflowers, asters, carrots & parsnips.

Antlike Flower Beetles (4)
About 160 species. Small elongated beetles, up to ½in long; move like ants. Black or brown, some with red or yellow markings. Found on flowers & leaves of trees & shrubs.

Many other beetles are also associated with flowers, including Scarabs (p. 31).

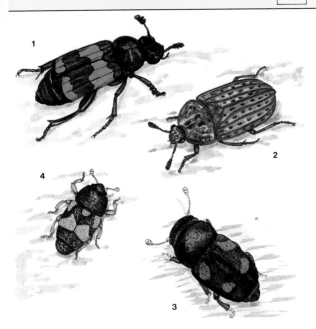

Carrion Beetles

About 40 species. Large, soft-bodied, flattened black beetles, ½–1½in, with red markings & clubbed antennae. Elytra loose or short & may expose rear of abdomen. Found throughout N. America. Most feed on carrion. **Sexton Beetles (1)** bury carrion & larvae feed on it underground. **Northern Carrion Beetles (2)** lay eggs in carcasses, where the larvae feed on the rotting flesh. Some species feed on decaying plants & may become pests in the garden, attacking vegetables, others eat fungi.

Sap Beetles

About 180 species, found in much of N. America. Oval, flattened, usually black beetles, ¼–½in long, often with red or yellow spots on elytra, like the **Red-spotted Sap Beetle (3)**. Antennae have distinct club formed of three segments. Adults & larvae feed on sap flows, nectar, carrion & fermenting fruits. Some live under bark of decaying logs, others in gardens on plants like hollyhocks, morning glories & hydrangeas. **Dried Fruit Beetles (4)** are pests in fruit stores.

These insects have two pairs of large, scale-covered wings, often with complex color patterns. Scales come off easily. Antennae knobbed in butterflies, simple or feathery in moths. Many have a long proboscis coiled beneath the head.

Most moths are nocturnal while butterflies fly by day. Many feed on nectar with their long proboscis which can reach far into flowers, others on sap or fermenting fruit.

Larvae are caterpillars; they have three pairs of legs on the thorax and usually five pairs of abdominal clasping prolegs. They feed by biting off sections of leaves and stems of plants and some do considerable damage. Many pupate in silken cocoon.

Butterfly wings are vertical when they rest; many are brightly colored. Skippers raise their fore wings and hold hind wings flat. Moths hold wings flat or in roof-like position; most are dull. Illustrated on this page are **Luna Moth** (1); **Alfalfa Looper** (2); **Hackberry Butterfly** (3); **Checkered White** (4).

1

Large, brightly colored butterflies, usually with long tails on the hind wings. They are striped in black and yellow or in black and white and many have blue and/or red spots on the hind wings. All three pairs of legs are fully developed.

Adults use their long proboscis to feed on nectar of flowers. Males patrol long distances searching for females or perch on plants in afternoon. They also gather at wet sand and water.

Caterpillars (1) usually smooth but some have tubercles; some resemble bird droppings, others are brightly colored. They can protrude a pair of odorous "horns" behind the head. They feed on citrus, pipevines and other plants.

Most swallowtails, like Anise and Black Swallowtails are multicolored. Pipevine Swallowtails are plain blue-black. Some individuals of **Tiger Swallowtails** (illustrated) and Spicebush Swallowtails mimic Pipevine Butterflies, which are distasteful to birds, and so gain protection from these predators.

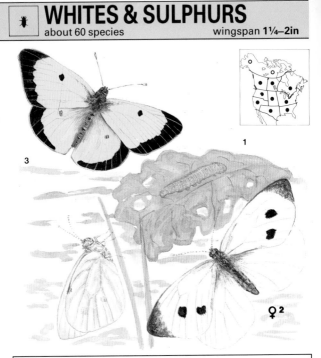

Small to medium-sized butterflies, white, yellow or orange in color, many with black markings. All six legs are fully developed.

Adults visit flowers for nectar or bask in the sun. Males patrol in search of females and visit wet sand or mud.

Caterpillars (1) cylindrical, smooth in texture, green in color often with longitudinal stripes. Caterpillars of whites feed on plants of the cabbage family; those of sulphurs feed on legumes. Some are pests. They do not make shelters.

Whites often have black markings or may be marbled yellow or green on the underside. Most familiar is the **Cabbage White** (2), a garden pest on brassicas. Orangetips are white with orange tips to their wings. Sulphurs, like the **Common Sulphur** (3), are yellow or orange, often with black margins.

Small blue, brown or copper-colored butterflies. Males have reduced fore legs so that only the two hind pairs are used in walking; all six legs are normally developed in females.

Adults fly rapidly, visiting a variety of flowers for nectar. Males patrol or perch on plants, searching for females; male blues gather at wet sand.

Caterpillars (1) flattened, slug-like, covered in fine hairs, broad in the middle and tapering front and back. Many produce honeydew from glands at the rear of the abdomen and are milked by ants. Feed on leaves, buds and flowers of many plants.

Male **blues** (2) may be seen patrolling for females (3) or visiting wet sand; female blues are brown with some blue markings. **Coppers** are orange-brown; males usually perch and watch for females (4). Hairstreaks are usually blue, gray or brown, mostly seen around trees or shrubs.

Medium-sized to large butterflies, brightly colored with complex patterns. Their fore legs are reduced to brush-like stumps in both sexes; the other legs are used for walking. Antennae are clothed with scales.

Adults fly well and males of many species patrol and search for females; others watch for them perched on bushes. They feed mostly on sap and fermenting fruit, also on nectar.

Caterpillars (1) often have several rows of tubercles with spiny hairs, and most have a pair of horns on the head. They feed mostly at night, on a variety of plants, shrubs and trees, hiding by day in shelters of folded or webbed leaves.

The largest and most diverse family of N. American butterflies, with many familiar representatives. They include the **Mourning Cloak** (2), Buckeye and Viceroy, as well as painted ladies, **fritillaries**, **checkerspots**, **admirals**, **anglewings** and tortoiseshells, like **Milbert's Tortoiseshell** (3).

BRUSH-FOOTED BUTTERFLIES

Fritillaries

Orange-brown butterflies with black spots & marks on the upper sides, many with silver spots on the lower sides of the wings, like the **Great Spangled Fritillary (1)**. Males patrol in search of females or visit mud puddles & carrion.

Checkerspots & Crescents

Black wings with a checkered pattern of yellow or orange gives these butterflies a distinctive look. Males patrol in search of females & perch in open areas. Adults, like the **Pearl Crescent (2)**, visit a wide variety of flowers.

Admirals

Black-winged butterflies with white stripe (White Admirals) or red stripe, like **Red Admiral (3)**, across both wings. Males often perch in afternoon & fly out at passing females. Adults feed at flowers & fermenting fruit.

Anglewings

Wings have ragged margins & tails on hind wings. There is a silver mark on underside of each hind wing. Adults feed on sap & fruit. Males perch in afternoon & watch for females. **Question Mark (4)** is common east of Rockies.

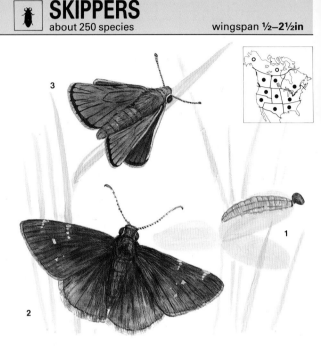

Small to medium-sized butterflies, black, brown or orange-brown in color, with large hairy bodies and relatively short wings for butterflies. Antennae thread-like with hooked tips.

Most adults fly with a characteristic direct, skipping flight. They visit flowers for nectar and also feed on fermenting fruits; males may also be seen at wet mud.

Caterpillars (1) are green, covered with many tiny hairs and have a distinct head; they taper front and back. They hide by day in shelters of silk-bound, rolled or folded leaves; many feed at night on grasses, others on a variety of other plants.

Some skippers, like the **Northern Cloudywing** (2), black dusky-wings and sootywings, spread their wings flat when at rest. Others, like the dark brown roadside skippers, orange **Garita Skipper** (3) and skipperlings, and orange and brown branded skippers, rest with fore wings raised and hind wings flat.

OTHER BUTTERFLIES

Milkweed Butterflies
Four species. Large bright orange-brown butterflies with black margins & veins. First pair of legs are stunted & knob-like. Antennae scaleless. These butterflies are poisonous because their larvae absorb poisons from milkweeds & pass them on to the adults. Found in south all year but **Monarchs (1)** migrate north to Canada in summer. **Queens (2)** remain mostly in south. They are mimicked by the Viceroy but this has a transverse black vein on hind wings.

Satyrs
50 species, throughout N. America. Dull brown or gray butterflies, often with eye-spots on wings, especially on underside. First pair of legs are reduced. They have an erratic, dancing flight close to the ground. Most satyrs stay close to their host plant, feeding on sap flows & fermenting fruit. Arctics are found in mountains & tundra; ringlets, like the **Prairie Ringlet (3)** in lowland & alpine meadows & woods; **wood nymphs (4)** in woods & forests. Their larvae feed on grasses.

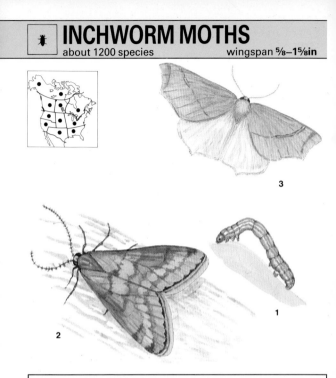

Small or medium-sized moths, with slender bodies and broad delicate wings, spread out flat when at rest. Hind and fore wings are similar, often with pattern continuing from one to the other. Antennae feathery in males, thread-like in females.

Nocturnal. Many are gray or brown with cryptic patterns on the wings so that they remain camouflaged during the day, pressed against the bark of a tree or a lichen-covered rock.

Caterpillars of many are twig-like inchworms (1); they move by extending the body and then drawing up the rear of the abdomen to form a loop. They feed on leaves of many different plants and may be seen hanging by silken threads from trees.

A large family, including grays and angles, cankerworms, spanworms, geometer moths, looper moths, emeralds, waves, carpets and blacks. **Fall Cankerworm** (2) larvae are pests on apples, and on other trees in eastern USA. **Calif. Spanworm** (3) larvae attack many shrubs and trees in western USA.

♂

3

2

1

Small or medium-sized moths with stout, furry bodies. Wings broad, white, yellow or red, many with black patterns or spots; held in roof-like position at rest. Female antennae thread-like, of males feathery with two branches per segment.

Adults may be nocturnal or active by day. Many are poisonous and the bright warning colors deter predators. Many do not feed at all, others feed on flower nectar.

Caterpillars very hairy; many are known as "woolly bears," (1). They feed on a variety of low-growing plants including lichens, grasses, dandelions and many others. Some are pests on trees like peaches, apples, poplars etc.

Many are plain or have a few spots on the wings, like **Isabella Tiger Moths** (2); others have bold wing patterns, like **Ornate Tiger Moths** (3). Lichen moths are yellow or dull gray moths whose larvae feed on lichens. Wasp moths mimic wasps but, unlike clearwing moths, they do not have transparent wings.

49

Medium-sized moths, with stout, usually hairy bodies. Mostly dull gray, brown or yellow with complex patterns on wings; hind wings often more brightly colored. At rest wings look triangular, flat or roof-like. Antennae usually thread-like.

Mostly nocturnal and often camouflaged to blend in with the background on which they rest by day. Many are attracted to lights at night. They often feed on fruit juices or sap.

Caterpillars (1) dull in color and hairless, usually striped or spotted; feed on leaves of wide variety of plants and trees. Some bore into stems and leaves, others (cutworms) hide in litter on the ground by day and attack plants at night.

The largest N. American moth family, including foresters, **daggers**, **darts**, **underwings**, **pinions**, looper moths, arches and others. Many, like **Armyworm Moth** (2) and cutworm moths have destructive larvae, pests of forest trees and crops. **Eight-spot Foresters** (3) may be seen in woods and cities.

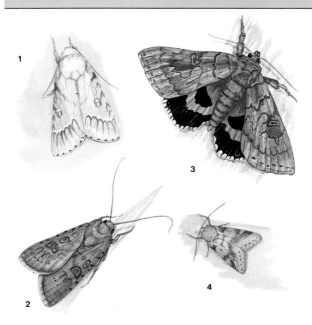

Dagger Moths (1)

Gray or brown moths, with white patterns on the wings & black marks or "daggers" on fore wings. Caterpillars found on wide variety of trees including oaks, apples, poplars, aspens, willows & maples.

Darts (2)

Usually brown with round & kidney-shaped spots or lines on fore wings. Larvae are cutworms, feeding on a variety of plants & crops like grasses, clovers, alfalfa, corn, tobacco, tomatoes & trees like maples & apples.

Underwings (3)

Fore wings camouflaged to resemble tree bark. Hind wings black, or banded in black & a bright color, exposed if moth is disturbed. Larvae are common on hickory, willows, oaks & other trees, also on blueberries & other plants.

Pinions & Sallows (4)

Mostly winter moths, flying in late fall & early spring; most common in the north. Yellow or brown in color with patterns of lines & spots. Larvae feed on many trees including apples, aspen, willows, maples & oaks.

SPHINX MOTHS

about 125 species

wingspan 1½–5½in

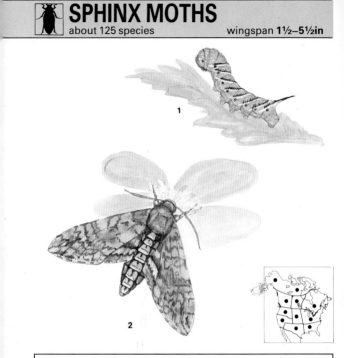

1

2

Medium-sized to large moths with heavy bodies and narrow, distinctively shaped, strong wings. Antennae thickened and spindle-shaped, with a bent tip which points upwards.

Adults are strong, fast fliers. They visit flowers for nectar, sipping it with their very long proboscis which is coiled beneath the head when not in use.

Caterpillars (1) stout and hairless with a large horn at the rear of the abdomen; they are often called hornworms. Feed on a wide variety of plants and trees and some are pests.

Also called hawk moths. Some fly by day and mimic bumble bees; others mimic hummingbirds, hovering in front of flowers while taking nectar. Others visit flowers at dusk. Pests include the **Carolina Sphinx** (2) whose caterpillars (tobacco or tomato hornworms) feed on potato, tomato and tobacco plants.

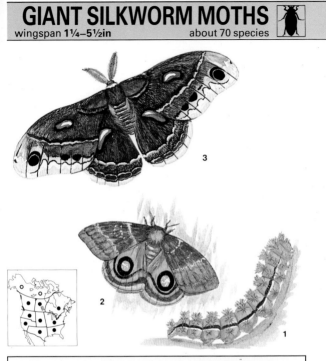

Large moths with stout hairy bodies and huge, often brightly colored wings with eyespots. Their antennae are feathery, with four branches per segment in males, two branches per segment in females. Proboscis reduced and very short, never coiled.

Adults most likely to be seen around street lights or lighted windows at night, but may also be active by day. They do not feed.

Caterpillars (1) grow large and fleshy, often with dense stinging hairs or tubercles; they usually feed on leaves of trees, like oaks, poplars and maples, and may do considerable damage. They pupate inside silk cocoon, like that of silkworm.

Io Moths (2) are likely to be found in open woods while Luna Moths are forest species. Cecropia Moths (3) fly in open ground, often in urban areas east of the Rockies. Promethea and Polyphemus Moths are both attracted to lights. True Silkworms are not native to N. America.

Snout Moths

About 1380 species, throughout N. America. Small or medium-sized moths, with a wingspan of ½–1½in. They often have large palps that project forwards or upwards, like a snout. Antennae simple. Fore wings resemble elongated triangles, hind wings broad. Many are pests: meal moths infest stored grain; **European Corn Borer** (1) larvae bore into corn, potatoes, beans, etc., cutting leaves off at the base & causing serious damage; **Sod Webworm Moth** (2) larvae are major lawn pests, east of the Rockies.

Tortricid Moths

About 350 species, throughout N. America. Small with broad, brownish or yellowish wings, which often widen suddenly at the base. Wingspan ⅜–1½in. Fore wings have square tips. Wings held in roof-like position at rest. Often pests in orchards & forests, on trees like apples, maples & oaks; larvae are leaf rollers or bore into stems and fruits. Spruce Budworm is a major pest in forests. **Codling Moth** (3) larvae bore into apples. **Orange Tortrix** (4) larvae are leaf-rollers on citrus trees.

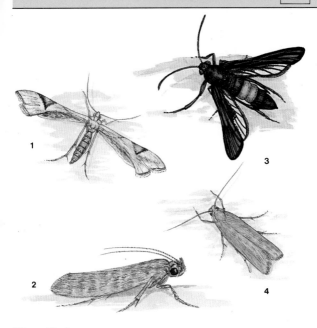

Plume Moths

About 150 species. Slender brown or gray moths. Narrow wings rolled together & held at right angles to body when at rest. Wings deeply lobed & fringed, plume-like. Larvae of **Artichoke Plume Moth** (**1**) feed on thistles & artichokes.

Gelechid Moths

About 630 species. Small, often iridescent, moths with narrow pointed fore wings. Hind wings have long tips. Larvae are leaf rollers or miners, form galls or eat seeds. Larvae of **Potato Tuberworm** (**2**) feed on potatoes.

Clearwing Moths

About 110 species. Day-flying moths often seen at flowers. They have transparent areas on wings, especially on hind wings. Many are wasp-mimics, with red or yellow striped abdomens. Larvae of **Peach Tree Borer** (**3**) are pests.

Clothes Moths (4)

About 175 species. Small brown or light-colored moths with a tuft of bristles on the head. Larvae of pest species feed on woolen clothes & carpets but many others feed on plant & animal remains in the wild.

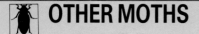

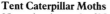

Tent Caterpillar Moths
35 species, in much of N. America. Medium-sized moths with stout hairy bodies & a wingspan of up to 4in. Wings shorter than body & held in a roof-like position when at rest. Antennae feathery with two branches to each segment. Eggs laid in ring around twigs in summer; hairy, brightly striped caterpillars emerge the following spring. The larvae (1) of **Eastern Tent Caterpillar Moths** (2) live in colonies in a silken tent; they are very destructive on apples & cherries.

Tussock Moths
About 30 species. Medium-sized moths, brown, gray or white in color. Antennae feathery. Caterpillars are hairy & have tufts of extra long hairs at front & back. Many are pests on forest trees. **Gypsy Moth** (3) larvae can defoliate whole areas of forest when numerous.

Prominents (4)
About 140 species. Medium-sized, brown or gray moths, resembling owlets, with stout bodies. Some are forest pests. Larvae may look like parts of plants. Some lift ends of body if disturbed.

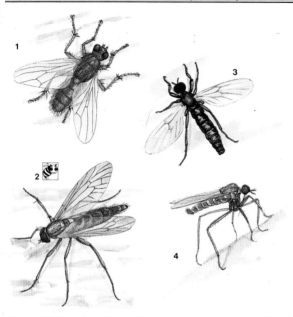

Soft-bodied or leathery insects, often covered with bristles. Head globular with large eyes, thorax oval and humpbacked. One pair of wings, the membranous fore wings. Hind wings modified as knob-like balancing organs. Antennae often small.

Adults found in many habitats, often around flowers searching for nectar; or near places where they lay their eggs, such as dung or carrion; or around larval hosts if they are parasites.

Larvae are soft legless grubs or "maggots," without well-defined heads. They adopt a variety of lifestyles. They may live in ponds, streams or soil; induce galls on plants; be parasites on other animals; or live in dung or carrion.

Flies include mosquitoes, midges, crane, horse, black, robber and soldier flies; also bee, hover, fruit, blow, house and parasitic flies and many others. Root and seed maggots are fly larvae. Illustrated on this page are **Dung Fly (1)**; **Snipe Fly (2)**; **March Fly (3)** and **Dance Fly (4)**.

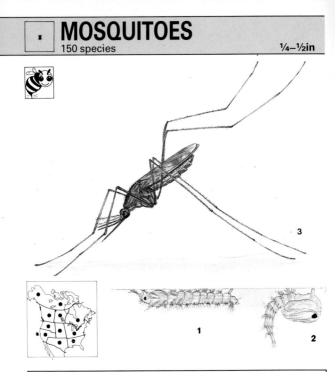

Slender, long-legged flies with a long, piercing proboscis with which females suck blood of people, mammals and birds. Males feed on nectar. Long antennae are feathery in male, hair-like in female. Hind legs are raised when they land.

Most likely to be found in damp places and most active at dusk and dawn. They occur in huge numbers in the north. Birds and dragonflies hunt and feed on mosquitoes.

Larvae are "wrigglers," (1) found in almost any small pond or puddle, ditches, streams etc. They may be seen, together with the pupae (2), hanging upside down from the water film when they come up for air. Feed on plankton.

Amongst the most familiar of the insects. Some are vectors of serious diseases, like the Yellow Fever Mosquito and **Malaria Mosquito** (3) found throughout much of central and eastern USA. Others, like the ubiquitous house mosquitoes, do not transmit disease but may spoil summer evening picnics.

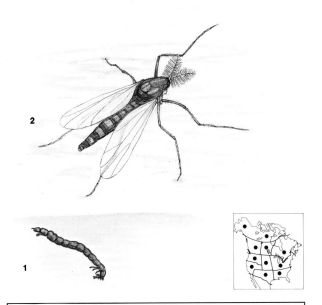

Small, fragile, slender flies without a long piercing proboscis and with wings held out to the sides when at rest. They alight with fore legs raised and often vibrating. Antennae of male feathery, of female hair-like.

Often appear in large swarms in late afternoon or at sunset near or above water. The swarms are mostly composed of males.

Larvae almost all aquatic, living in streams, rivers and ponds, often making a tube in mud at the bottom. They are soft-bodied and worm-like, some are bright red bloodworms (**1**). Often used as bait and an important food for fishes.

Common Midges (**2**) may be attracted to lights at night. The larvae of some species are indicative of polluted water. **Mosquitoes,** with which midges are often confused, have a long, piercing proboscis, wings folded over the back when at rest and hind legs raised when they alight.

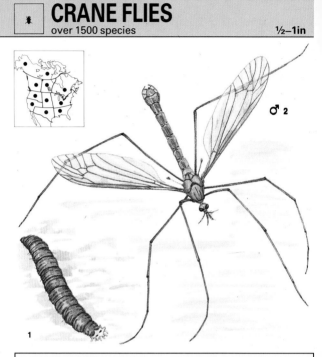

♂ 2

1

Like giant, brownish mosquitoes with very long legs which come off easily, clumsy in movement and in flight. There is a prominent V-shaped line on the thorax between the wings. Some have brown spots on wings. They do not bite.

Abundant in a wide variety of habitats from grasslands to woods, marshes and gardens and may come into houses. Most common in damp areas where larvae are abundant in the soil.

Larvae are "leatherjackets" (1) and live in soil, especially in wet places and marshes, feeding on decaying plants or on roots of grasses and of other plants. Some live in streams and ponds. They may be garden pests but provide food for birds.

Crane flies are all similar in form and habits and difficult to identify. **Range Crane Flies** (2) may occur in huge numbers in the west where their larvae may damage grains. Winter crane flies are similar but belong to another family. They appear in large swarms in winter and spring.

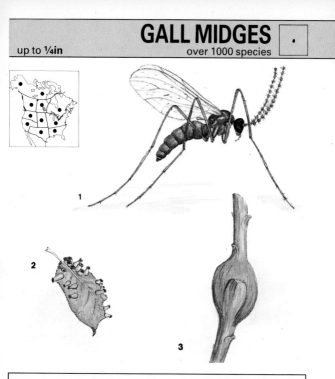

Tiny slender, fragile flies with long legs. Wings with less than seven longitudinal veins reaching the wing margins. Antennae of some species have characteristic whorls of tiny sensory hairs.

Flies are less likely to be seen than their effects on plants; distorted flowers and buds; tumor-like galls on stems, leaves or twigs; or reduced seed yield when fruits are affected.

Larvae tiny, short and stout, orange, pink or yellow. About half of them induce gall formation on plants. Others live in rotting plant material or fungi (some are pests on mushrooms), others are predators or live in nests of ants or termites.

Most attack native plants and trees, like **Juneberry Gall Flies (1)** which induce pyramidal galls on Juneberry leaves (2); or **Golden Rod Gall Flies** which induce tumor-like galls (3) on golden rod stems. Some, like Hessian Flies, attack crops; the larvae bore into stems of cereals causing considerable losses.

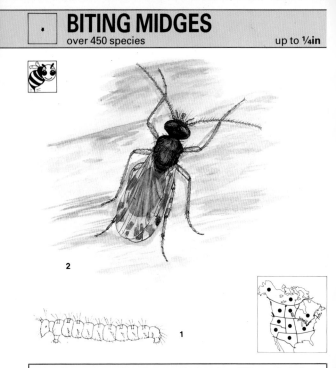

2

1

Tiny flies with small heads and quite long legs. Wings relatively large and folded flat over back when insect is at rest. Proboscis encloses six cutting blades for biting. Only females bite, males can be identified by feathery antennae.

May occur in huge numbers near beaches, streams and ponds, biting by day with painful bites. Many prey on other insects, midges, dragonflies, butterflies, sucking blood and juices.

Larvae (**1**) slender and wormlike, aquatic or semi-aquatic, living in a variety of habitats from moist earth to tree holes, in wet decaying vegetation or on oceanic beaches.

Also called punkies or no-see-ums because they are so small. The bites of Black Valley Gnats and other biting midges cause itching and swelling in early summer in Calif. and the southwest. **Saltmarsh Punkies** (**2**) cause similar problems in the south and east; their larvae live in saltmarshes.

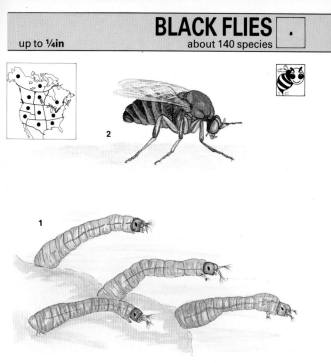

Very small, stout, black or gray flies; their short legs are often marked with yellow. They have short antennae, humped backs and proportionately large wings with broad bases. Females bite mammals, birds and people, males do not bite.

These flies are common in spring and early summer, especially in woodland and near running water. They can be a considerable nuisance and can be dangerous to livestock if numerous.

Larvae (1) are attached in groups to rocks in fast-flowing water, by sucking disks near the tail and by a silken line. Feed on micro-organisms drawn by a water current, created by fans on the head. Larvae pupate in underwater cocoons.

Also known as buffalo gnats. Many **black flies**, like the species illustrated (2), torment and bite people; they are most abundant near water, in the north and in the mountains. Turkey Gnats are pests attacking turkeys and other birds throughout the USA.

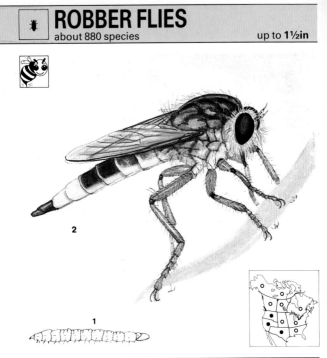

2

1

Either long, slender, hairless flies or short, hairy, bee-like flies, all with long bristly legs. Usually dull-colored, gray or black. Eyes very large, on a broad, flattened head. Face bearded with a piercing proboscis; they may bite if handled.

They hunt insects like grasshoppers, wasps, bees. Some have a favorite perch and fly out at victims, others patrol on the wing. Prey collapse when bitten, probably poisoned.

Larvae (1) are cylindrical in form with two long hairs on each side of the thorax. They live in the soil, under bark of decaying wood or in leaves, and feed on larvae of other insects; some of their prey are pests like beetle larvae.

The majority occur in southwestern USA. Most species are limited to a small area and habitat. Most are beneficial, like the **Bearded Robber Fly (2)** from the southern USA, feeding on pests like beetles, flies and grasshoppers. However Bee Killers can cause damage to hive bees.

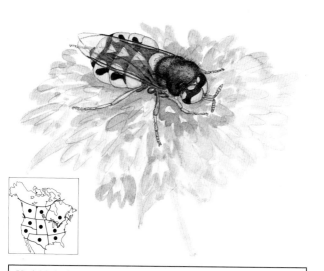

Variable in form, from stout to slender, even sometimes wasp-like, with broad flat abdomen wider than folded wings. Many are green, yellow or blue, others black with green or yellow markings on the abdomen. They are covered in short fine hair.

Most often seen on flowers in meadows or on woodland edges. Larger ones are slow, poor fliers and often rest on plants but the smaller Sargus Soldier Flies hover in the air.

Larvae variable in their habits. Many are aquatic, others live in damp soil, decaying wood or rotting plant debris, moss, dung or under stones. Some feed on plant material, others are carnivores. They are often parasitized by chalcid wasps.

Black soldier flies are found in farms and around houses and their larvae live in manure and decaying vegetation. **Common soldier flies** (illustrated), together with yellow and Sargus soldier flies are all associated with flowers of the carrot family like Wild Parsley, Wild Parsnip and Hemlock.

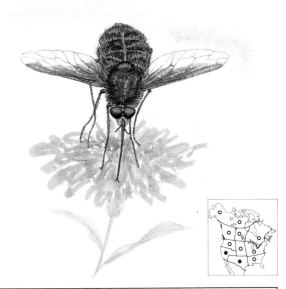

Stout, furry flies like quick, active bumblebees. They have long legs, proboscis-like mouthparts and clouded or patterned wings which are held outstretched when at rest. Vary in color from brown or black to yellow or white. They do not bite.

May be seen hovering motionless except for the rapid vibration of the wings, quickly darting away if disturbed. Above bare ground, around flowers, or resting on leaves or on the ground.

Crescent-shaped larvae vary in habit; some are predaceous on beetle larvae and grasshopper eggs, others are parasites on moths, bees, wasps and beetle larvae. Still others live in the nests of bees.

Many species are found only in sandy, arid areas of the south west; they are mostly absent from the colder, wetter areas, few are present in the north. **Large bee flies** (illustrated) occur throughout most of the continent; they frequent flowers in meadows and gardens, especially in sandy areas.

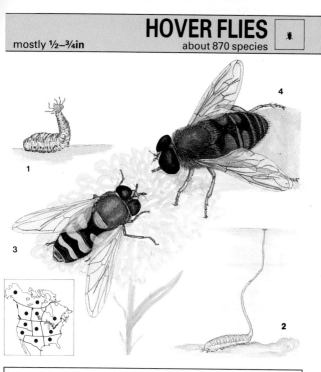

Hover flies are often striped in black and yellow or resemble bees. They have a distinctive false vein on each wing that does not link up with any other vein. The large eyes occupy a large part of the head. Proboscis short and fleshy.

Quick, active flies that dart from place to place or hover in mid air. Usually seen around flowers where they feed on pollen and nectar; they are important pollinators.

Many larvae are highly beneficial, feeding on aphids (**1**) and scale insects; others are aquatic, like rat-tailed maggots (**2**); some live in nests of bees, wasps and ants; a few attack bulbs. They look like tiny slugs with a pointed front end.

Many hover flies, like the **American Hover Fly** (**3**), mimic wasps or bees and may avoid predators in this way; they are harmless. **Drone flies** (**4**), the adults of rat-tailed maggots, resemble bees. Larvae of bulb flies are scavengers which also attack bulbs of onions and daffodils, making them soft.

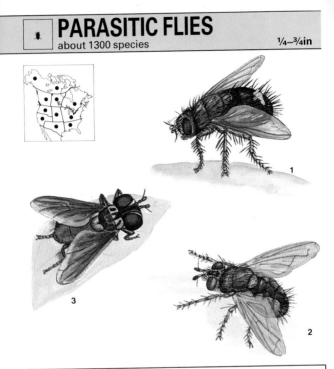

Large, stout flies with many large bristles, especially on the back of the abdomen. They have a large swelling on the thorax, best seen from the side of the fly. Adults make a loud buzzing noise in flight. They are strong fliers.

Adults are found in a wide variety of habitats from meadows, fields and gardens to woods and forests. They visit flowers to feed on nectar and pollen.

Larvae live as parasites inside insects like beetle and sawfly larvae, caterpillars, nymphs of grasshoppers and bugs. Eggs are laid on leaves to be eaten by caterpillars or laid on or inserted into the host. Larvae develop inside the living host.

Along with parasitic wasps, parasitic flies are largely responsible for controlling insect populations. They control pests like caterpillars, locusts, weevil larvae, wood-boring beetles and many other insects. Species illustrated are parasitic on caterpillars (1) and (2) and on squash bugs (3).

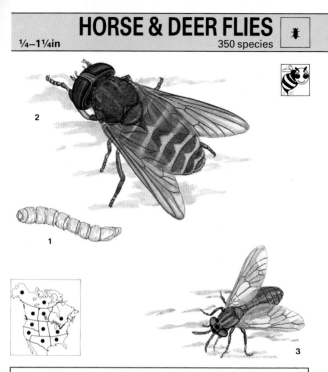

Quite large, bristleless flies, many with large iridescent green, brown or purple eyes. They vary in color from pale yellow to brown or black, usually with stripes on the abdomen. Females pester and bite people, horses, cattle and deer.

Females fly silently and bite savagely; often fly in circles around head of victim before landing. Most abundant in summer and fall. Males feed on nectar and are not often seen.

Larvae (1) large, rounded in cross-section and pointed at both ends. Found in damp places, in decaying logs, in soil, under stones or in water. Predaceous, hunting worms and insect larvae.

Horse flies (2) are up to an inch long, black or brown; one eastern species (Greenhead) has green eyes, others have gray or black eyes. **Deer flies (3)** are most common in lowland marshes and mountains; they are up to half an inch long, with black and yellow markings, often with green or gold eyes.

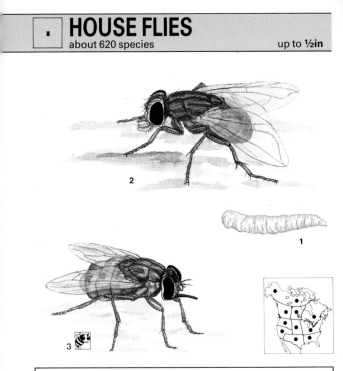

Stout, active flies, usually gray or brown, sometimes black or yellow, with a broad lobe at the base of each wing. Although they are generally bristly, there are no bristles around the wing bases on the thorax.

Adults found around houses and farms, where they feed on dung and excreta, nectar and exposed foods.

Larvae (1) develop in a variety of habitats. They may live inside plants, in decaying vegetation, manure and dung, also in carrion and garbage. Some are aquatic.

Common House Flies (2) are vectors for several diseases like typhoid, dysentery, cholera and worms, which they carry on their feet; they do not bite. **Stable Flies** (3) bite; they are found around farms and fields. Their larvae develop in piles of decaying straw, vegetation and manure.

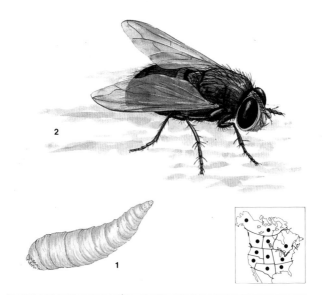

Metallic blue, green or black, bristly flies with a large lobe at the base of each wing. There is no swelling on the thorax such as is seen in parasitic flies. These flies buzz loudly in flight.

Adults feed on rotting plants and carrion and are often found in large numbers around such materials. Also attracted to fresh meat and open wounds. They feed also on pollen.

Larvae (1) develop from eggs laid in carrion, rotting vegetation and dung; a few are intestinal parasites. They will also develop in meat or wounds if allowed, keeping the wound sterile but unhealed.

Bluebottles (2) are common household and farmyard pests, laying eggs on exposed meat and other foods. Screw-worm flies lay eggs in the skin of cattle and other mammals and the larvae attack cuts on hatching and create open sores; these are pests in many areas of the USA.

71

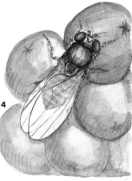

Peacock Flies

About 280 species, found in much of N. America. Small, multi-colored flies, up to ½in long, with elaborate patterns on body & wings. The males behave in a distinctive fashion, strutting about on leaves while opening & closing their wings; this is courtship display for females. Larvae (1) are white maggots found in nuts, fruits, leaves & stems of many plants; many of these flies are highly damaging pests. They include **Apple Maggots** (2), cherry fruit flies, gooseberry fruit flies & parsnip leaf miners.

Pomace Flies

About 120 species, found in much of N. America. Small yellow or brown flies, about ¼in long, many with red eyes. They are common around rotting & fermenting fruit where they feed on yeasts; they also feed on flower nectar, sap & fungi. The larvae (3) are whitish maggots which burrow into the fermenting fruit & feed on yeasts & bacteria. **Laboratory Fruit Flies** (4) are used in studies on heredity because they have a short life cycle, only about two weeks from egg to adult.

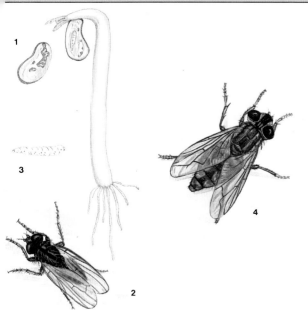

Root and Seed Maggots

Over 400 species, in much of N. America. Slender, dark flies, about ⅜in long, like houseflies with long legs. Adults hunt other insects. Many larvae (or maggots) feed on decaying plants, but others are pests. **Seed Maggots** (1) attack planted seeds of many crops, including wheat, beans, corn, potatoes, melons etc. **Onion Maggot Flies** (2), Cabbage Maggots, Beet Leaf Miners & Raspberry Cane Borers lay eggs in soil. Larvae (3) bore into roots of affected plants & damage or kill them.

Flesh Flies (4)

About 330 species, throughout N. America. Large gray or black flies, up to 1in long, like non-metallic blowflies, often with yellow bristles. Adults feed on fruit juices, nectar, sap & aphid honeydew. Males are territorial & fly out at females from their look-out posts. Many larvae develop in carrion, raw meat, open wounds or dung; others are parasites on grasshoppers, beetles & in vertebrates; some develop in wasp nests & some are aquatic predators in pitcher plants.

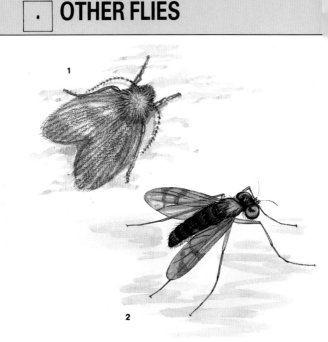

Moth Flies (1)

90 species. Tiny hairy flies like small moths, about ¼in long. The wings are broad & often held in a roof-like position over the back when the insect is at rest. They are weak fliers. Nocturnal in habit, they may be attracted to lights at night & enter homes. Found in much of N. America, near drains & sewers, also in damp shady places. Larvae are semi-aquatic & feed on decaying plant remains or detritus in drains, sinks & sewers.

Long-legged Flies (2)

About 1220 species. Small, slender flies, up to ¼in long, with long legs & often with metallic green or copper-colored abdomens. Males have tufts of scales, especially on legs, which they show off when courting females. Adults common in wet meadows, marshes & along streams, throughout N. America, where they hunt small insects. They may be seen skating on the water surface or on leaves. Larvae live in water, moist soil or under bark, hunting small insects.

Shore and Seaweed Flies
There are about 430 species of **shore flies** (**1**), small dark flies, up to ⅜in long, which may be present in large numbers on the water surface at edges of ponds, streams, marshes, brackish & tidal pools on the coast. They feed on other insects trapped in the water film. The five species of **seaweed flies** (**2**) are flattened, bristly flies, up to ⅜in long. They are found, often in large numbers, in stranded seaweed on beaches of both coasts.

Frit Flies (**3**)
About 270 species. Very small, stout, almost hairless flies, up to ¼in long, either dark gray or black & yellow. There is a large dark shining triangle on the front of the face. Adults are common in grassland & on low plants. Larvae feed on decaying vegetation & grasses, or form galls; others feed on aphids & insect eggs. Eye Gnats are a considerable nuisance in much of N. America, attempting to enter eyes & may transmit eye diseases.

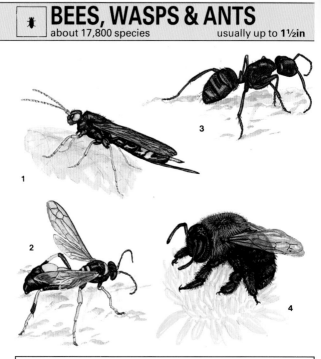

Soft or hard-bodied, often elongated insects. They have two pairs of membranous wings, joined to look like one pair. A row of hooks at the front of the smaller hind wing engages into a groove on the back of the fore wing. Antennae quite long.

Most are solitary but some are social, living in colonies. Many are essential pollinators of flowers. Parasitic species regulate insect numbers throughout the land.

Larvae parasitic on other insects, gall-makers or feed on plants. Free-living plant feeders resemble caterpillars; they are often pests. Others are white, grub-like without legs and rarely seen since they are concealed in host, gall or nest.

Sawflies and horntails have no waist. Other species all have a distinct waist between the thorax and abdomen: these include the wasps, bees, ants and ichneumons. Illustrated on this page are **Horntail Wasp (1); Black and Yellow Mud Dauber (2); Carpenter Ant (3); Carpenter Bee (4).**

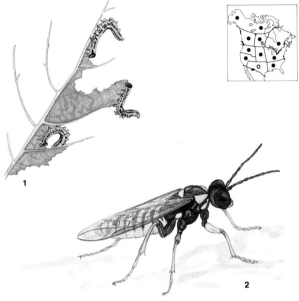

1

2

Black or brown wasp-like insects, some with red or yellow markings; however they do not have a waist-like division between thorax and abdomen. Females have saw-like ovipositor. Antennae long and thread-like.

Adults found around the larval food plants or visiting flowers, searching for nectar.

Larvae (1) resemble caterpillars. On leaves they may do much damage, especially if they live in groups when they can reduce leaves to skeletons. Some are leaf rollers, others are leaf miners; some induce galls; others attack flowers or fruits.

Sawflies are pests on trees like ash, spruce and larch; **Northeastern Sawfly** (2) larvae feed on willows and other riverside trees. Others attack fruits of apples and pears, making them drop off the tree. Sawflies also attack raspberries, grapes and roses, and native plants like grasses, sedges and ferns.

Small bees, usually with a black or brown abdomen and densely hairy head and thorax. There is a pollen brush present on each hind leg. They are short-tongued and so visit short-tubed and open flowers where they can reach the nectar and pollen.

Important pollinators, especially for spring flowers like willows and fruit blossoms, later for plants like evening primroses, milkweeds, Californian Lilac, blackberries.

Mostly solitary. Females dig burrows in spring, leading to branching brood chambers; they may be numerous in sandy ground or on dirt trails. Entrance is tiny hole, at first surrounded by small pile of dirt. Larvae emerge following spring.

The many species of **mining bees** (illustrated) are difficult to distinguish from each other. Sweat bees, with which they may be confused, are small brown or black bees, often with a metallic green thorax; they are important pollinators. Some are attracted to sweat and will sting if trapped in clothing.

Small to medium-sized, dark-colored, stout-bodied, hairy bees. They carry pollen on the hairy underside of the abdomen which often looks yellow as a consequence. They are long-tongued and have sharp, biting mouthparts.

These important pollinators may be seen visiting a wide variety of flowers. Leaf-cutting bees cut segments from leaves or petals of many plants, including roses and willows.

Mostly solitary. Some make nests consisting of row of cells in a hole, others make nests under stones, in rotten wood or soil or attach a cell to a tree branch. Female provisions each cell with bee-bread for the larva, which emerges following year.

Leaf-cutting bees (1) line the cells of their nests with cut pieces of leaves. **Mason bees (2)** use mud and clay to build their cells or nests; resin bees use resin. Some bees of this family are parasites on the others, laying their own eggs in the nests of others and removing the original eggs.

BUMBLE BEES
about 50 species

3/4–1 1/4in

1

2

Mostly large, robust, hairy bees, usually black with yellow, sometimes red markings. Pollen collected in "baskets" on broad hind legs to take back to hive. They have long tongues which can reach into long-tubed flowers. Will sting if provoked.

Most likely to be seen around flowers collecting pollen for pollen baskets. Important pollinators of many plants that other insects cannot pollinate, including alfalfa and clovers.

Social. Queens emerge in spring to start colonies in the ground, often in a hole. Colony at first consists of queen and female workers who make growing nest of cells containing larvae; male drones and young queens are produced later.

Common species include **Red-tailed Bumble Bee** (**1**), Western and **American Bumble Bee** (**2**). Usurper bumble bees lack pollen baskets on their legs; their queens parasitize other bumble bee nests, killing the rightful queens and laying their own eggs. The similar **carpenter bees** lack colored markings.

½in (workers); up to ¾in (queen)

Hairy brown bees with dark head and thorax, dull orange bands on the abdomen and a black "tail." There is a pollen basket on each hind leg. The sting of these bees is barbed and they can sting only once and then die.

Workers (illustrated) are pollinators for many trees, plants and crops. Seen around flowers collecting pollen. Most live in man-made hives and produce honey and wax.

Social. Hive consists of queen and sterile workers, larvae and pupae, and males at some times of year. Swarm occurs when old queen leaves with most of workers, searching for a hole for a new nest. Young queen will rebuild old colony, after mating.

Honey bees all belong to one species, although there are several varieties. Hive bees were originally European honey bees. Wild forms exist in other parts of the world. **Bumble bees** are much larger with characteristic colored markings; **carpenter bees** are black with shiny abdomens.

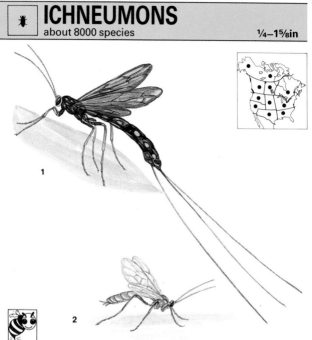

Slender, wasp-like insects often with a very long abdomen.
Female often has long ovipositor protruding from end of body.
The black antennae are often marked with white or yellow and
vibrate constantly; they are at least as long as the body.

Almost all are parasites on other insects, controlling their
numbers throughout much of the continent. Most are found in
wetter areas and they are rarer in arid regions.

Larvae are parasites, mostly developing in other insect larvae and
pupae, some in spiders. Hosts include caterpillars, larvae of wood-
boring and leaf-mining beetles and flies amongst others. Female
can detect host in tree or wood.

More than half of the species are unnamed. Many are brightly
colored in black or brown and yellow; others plain. Some of the
largest may sting if caught, although most do not. Many have a
long abdomen and ovipositor, like the **Giant Ichneumons (1)**, but
others do not, like **short-tailed ichneumons (2)**.

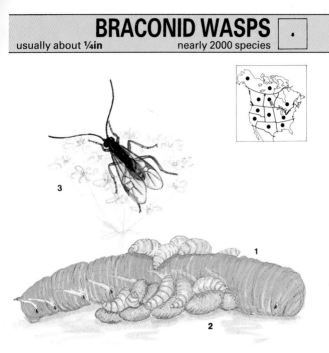

These insects are like miniature ichneumons, but are stouter in form with rounded instead of slender abdomens; they have a long slender ovipositor. Dark in color, brown or black, without colored markings and with long, plain dark antennae.

Adults are active but inconspicuous insects which may be seen on flowers, especially of the parsley family. Females may be seen around larvae of other insects, especially caterpillars.

Larvae (1) are parasites in insects, mostly in larvae of moths, butterflies, flies or beetles; many of the tiny braconid larvae may develop inside a single host. They emerge to pupate in cocoons (2) outside the dead host.

Braconids provide controls on many insect numbers. **Apanteles** (3) species are parasites on caterpillars, including those of **Cabbage Whites** and **Gypsy Moths**, and are used for biological control of these pests. The related aphid wasps parasitize aphids; the larvae pupate in mummified bodies of their hosts.

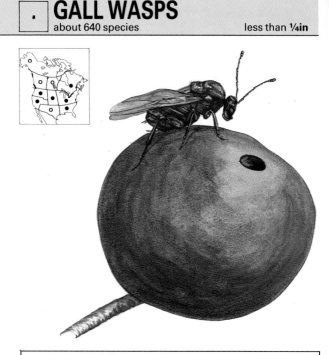

Very small, humpbacked wasps, usually black, brown or yellowish. They have a shiny, shortened abdomen, flattened from side to side. Antennae are long and not elbowed.

Adults fly in spring and fall but they are far less likely to be seen than the galls they induce on plants, mostly on oaks, but also on plants from the rose and daisy families.

Eggs laid on plants induce the formation of a swelling or gall and the larvae develop inside. One or many may be present. Some species lay their eggs on existing galls, their larvae develop as "guests" and may destroy original inhabitants.

About 480 species of these wasps induce galls on oaks. Galls vary from malformed buds, to flat stars and cones on leaves, to oak apples. **Calif. Oak Apple Wasp** (illustrated) induces largest and most familiar western gall on a variety of oaks. Jumping Oak Galls fall off and move as the larvae move inside.

Very small, parasitic wasps with short, elbowed antennae. The veins on the wings are reduced to a single vein along the front of the fore wing. Black, dark blue or green in color, many of them metallic.

Together with the parasitic flies, these wasps provide the most important controls on insect populations on the continent. They occur wherever their hosts are present.

Larvae are mostly parasites of other insects. Females insert eggs into eggs or larvae of a huge variety of insects, including flies, beetles, bees and moths and the parasitic larva develops inside the host, killing it.

Over 2000 species of chalcids are known at present. Most are parasites, like the one illustrated. The larvae of fairyflies, the smallest insects (adults are less than one sixteenth of an inch long), develop inside eggs of other insects. Equally small Trichogramma flies are used to control greenhouse pests.

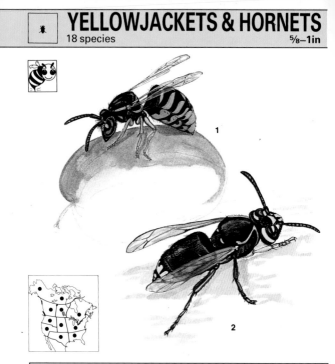

1

2

Black and yellow or black and white wasps with a distinct waist between thorax and abdomen. They fold their wings longitudinally when at rest. They have the ability to inflict a severe sting which can be repeated over and over again.

Workers forage for food amongst flowers and garbage cans; they may be pests in homes and at picnic sites when they are attracted to sweet foods and meat. Also hunt other insects.

Social. Queens start nests in spring, at first with queen and female workers only. Hornet nests hang in trees, wasp nests are built underground. They are papery in texture, with cells containing larvae; males and young queens are produced later.

Yellowjackets (1) are striped in yellow and black; they are ubiquitous pests. **Bald-faced Hornet** (2) is black with pale yellow-white markings on face and abdomen, most likely to be seen on flowers. The brown and yellow Giant Hornet is a forest species. Paper wasps are reddish-brown, circled with yellow.

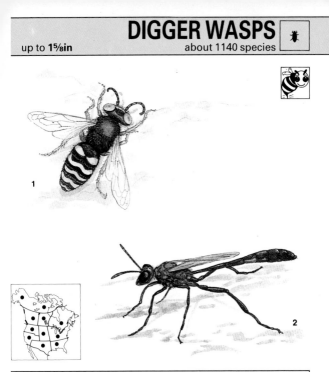

Quite large wasps with a slender waist between thorax and abdomen, usually black or brown with various markings. Their wings are not folded over the abdomen when they are at rest. There is a characteristic "collar" at the back of the head.

Adults may be seen at flowers where they feed on nectar and catch small insects. They may also be found digging their burrows or hunting for prey for the larvae.

Solitary hunting wasps. Females of most species make a burrow in the ground, kill or paralyze their prey and leave it in the burrow with their eggs for their larvae to feed on. Prey include caterpillars, grasshoppers and small spiders.

Sand wasps (1) nest in groups, making mounds in sandy ground or in gravels, and using flies as their larval prey. **Thread-waisted wasps** (2) are seen along paths and roads, they use stones to tamp down soil over their burrows. **Mud daubers** build mud nests on buildings or in soil, and may be seen at wet mud.

Spider Wasps

About 290 species, in much of N. America. Long-legged black or blue wasps, ½–2in long, with dark wings held lengthwise over back when at rest. Female antennae usually curled. Can inflict a very painful sting. Usually seen at flowers or hunting on the ground for spiders; they flick their wings as they run. Spiders are stung & paralyzed, dragged into branched tunnel, one spider to each branch. An egg is laid on each spider. **Tarantula hawks** (1) are large species found in southern USA.

Cuckoo Wasps (2)

About 230 species. Brilliant, metallic blue or green, hard-bodied wasps which do not sting. They may curl into a ball if disturbed. Most likely to be seen at rocks, walls & fences looking for burrows of other solitary wasps & bees, in many parts of N. America. They are parasites with a cuckoo-like life-style: they lay eggs in burrows of other wasps & bees. Their larvae kill the original larvae and feed on them and their stored prey. Some attack sawfly larvae and walkingstick eggs.

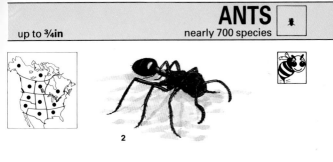

2

1

Small red, brown or black insects with first segments of abdomen narrowed into nodular waist. Antennae elbowed. Fertile males and females are winged forms which swarm; workers are wingless. Most bite if disturbed, some sting.

Ants are often scavengers and some become pests in homes and picnic sites where they are attracted to sugary foods. Some tend and defend aphids, and milk them for their honeydew.

Social. Nest made in soil, of piles of sticks and pine needles or in rotten wood. Consists of queen and workers; some species also have soldiers. At certain times of year small winged males and large winged females swarm; females start new nests.

Red Ants (1) are aggressive and defend nests and aphids. **Fire Ants (2)** may be pests in homes and gardens; they build large mounds and have painful stings. Carpenter ants nest in tree stumps and wood; they may damage buildings. Little Black Ants are common in homes throughout much of N. America.

Small to medium-sized insects with two pairs of wings. Fore wings partly horny and colored, with membranous tips. At rest fore wings are held flat over the back and cover hind wings. Membranous tips of fore wings then overlap.

Bugs have mouthparts modified for sucking; they suck the sap of plants, or hunt other insects, piercing their prey and sucking out the juices. Some are parasites, sucking blood.

Nymphs are usually like small adults but wingless. External wing buds gradually enlarge with each of the five molts. Nymphs have similar lifestyle to adults, with sucking mouthparts which remain the same throughout their life.

Many bugs live and feed on plants, including **stilt bugs** (1), **negro bugs** (2), plant, lace, seed, squash and stink bugs. Others are predators like ambush bugs. **Bed bugs** (3) are parasites, sucking blood from people. Others are aquatic like **toe-biters** (4), water boatmen and water striders.

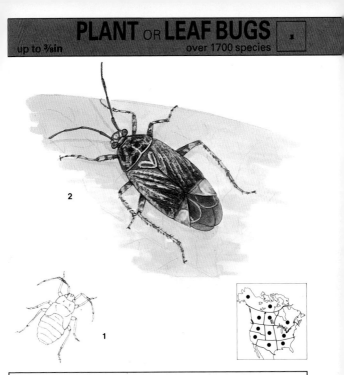

Fragile bugs, usually elongated or oblong in outline. Fore wings have two distinctive looped veins in the membranous area. Some are brightly colored while others are camouflaged in green or brown. Their legs come off easily.

Found on plants and may be pests. The majority feed on plants; most are restricted to one species of plant but a few are more widespread. Some are predators on other insects.

Nymphs (1) similar to adults, lose legs easily like adults and lead a similar life. They often have disproportionately long antennae. Wing buds develop externally, enlarging with each molt until with the final molt they become wings.

The biggest bug family in N. America. Pests include Suckfly on tobacco, Tomato Bug, Onion Plant Bug, Pear Plant Bug, Four-lined Plant Bug which is a pest on garden crops. Scarlet plant bugs and **Tarnished Plant Bug** (2) are found on a variety of crops, native and garden plants.

91

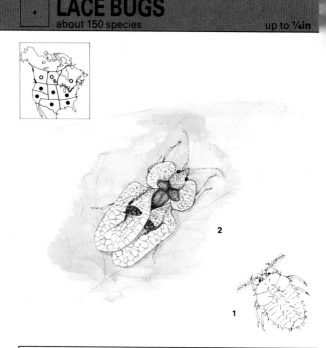

2

1

Small flattened, distinctive bugs in which the thorax and fore wings look like lacework and are often considerably expanded. Many are grayish in color and they are often covered with wax.

Found on herbaceous plants, shrubs and trees and often cause considerable damage, discoloration and whitening of the leaves. They live on the undersides of the leaves.

Eggs are laid in plant tissues, often in the midrib of a leaf and covered with viscid cones which soon harden. Nymphs (1) have a similar life style to the adults and are often found with them; they are often spiny and much darker than adults.

Pests include **Sycamore Lace Bug** (2) and Oak Lace Bug, both of which are pests on their host trees. Lace bugs are also found on apples, azaleas, elms, hackberries, cotton, eggplants, chrysanthemums and other plants.

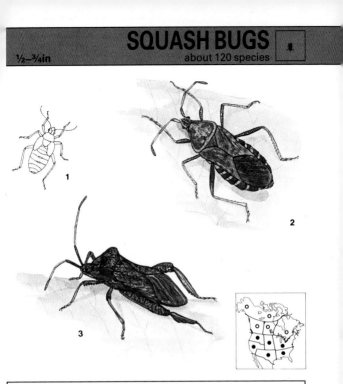

Large, often rather elongated bugs, usually brown or gray in color, with many veins on the membranous area of the fore wings. Head narrow, eyes large. Often exude a foul-smelling liquid if disturbed.

These bugs feed on plants, often on fruits and seeds, and some are serious crop pests. They are found on their host plants.

Nymphs (1) are similar to adults but wingless and they may have very long antennae. Their wing buds enlarge gradually with each molt. They are found in the same places as the adults.

The majority of species are found in the south and southwest. The **Squash Bug** (2), found throughout most of N. America, may be a serious pest on squashes. The hind legs of the **leaf-footed bugs** (3) are widened, often resembling leaves. Cactus bugs attack cactuses in the southwest.

93

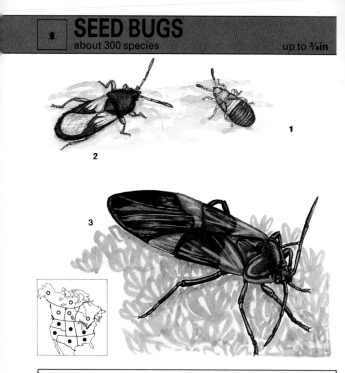

Very diverse group of elongated or oval, hard-bodied bugs; many are dull brown or yellow but others are strikingly colored. They have only five distinct veins in the membranous area of each fore wing.

Most feed on the seeds of grasses and other plants or suck plant juices; some prey on other insects. They are found in meadows, fields and crops, especially amongst grasses.

Nymphs (1) are similar to adults but wingless. Their wing buds enlarge gradually with each molt. They lead similar lives to the adults and are found in the same places.

The **Chinch Bug** (2) is a notorious pest on corn and other grains and causes serious losses. False Chinch Bug is sometimes a pest on fruits. Few of the other species are pests and big-eyed bugs are useful predators. **Milkweed bugs** (3) are brightly colored and used in laboratories.

1

2

Large, broad-bodied, shield-shaped bugs, many green or brown but some with bright markings. There is a large triangular dorsal shield between the wings. They have large scent glands on the underside which can exude a foul-smelling liquid.

Found on all kinds of vegetation, many feeding on plant juices, others hunting other insects. Some are important predators on plant pests.

Eggs barrel-shaped and laid in clusters. Young nymphs (1) are ladybird-shaped and remain in clusters near eggs. They become flatter and squarer as they molt and tend to scatter. They have no dorsal shield and so look rather different to adults.

Spined soldier bugs are common predatory stink bugs. Two-spotted Stink Bug, brightly colored with yellow markings, feeds on eggs of Colorado Potato Beetle. Many plant-sucking species are green like the green stink bugs found in orchards. **Harlequin Cabbage Bug** (2) feeds on cabbages.

95

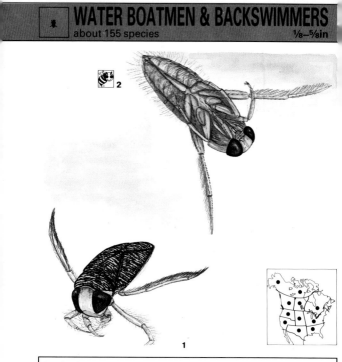

1

Backswimmers look like boats with a pair of oars; they swim on their backs and have large flattened hind legs which they use like oars. They may bite if handled. Water Boatmen use both hind and middle legs as oars and swim the right way up.

Found in still waters of ponds and lakes. Backswimmers rest at the surface, head down with abdomen projecting into air. Water Boatmen cling to rocks or weeds and stay close to bottom.

Nymphs similar to adults and with similar life style, but smaller. Wing buds develop externally, enlarging with each molt until with the final molt they become wings.

There are about 120 species of **water boatmen** (**1**) and 35 species of **backswimmers** (**2**). Other aquatic bugs include the **toe-biters**, water scorpions and creeping water bugs; these all have enlarged saber-like front legs with which they catch their prey.

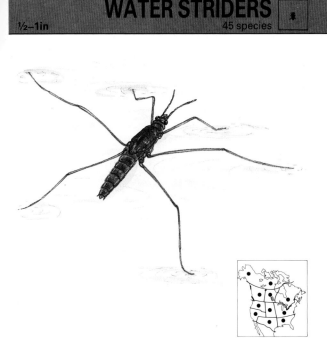

Bugs with long bodies and long middle and hind legs, which rest on the water making little dimples on the surface. The body is covered in thick velvety, waterproof hair which stops the insects from becoming trapped in the water.

Semi-aquatic insects which "skate" on the water of ponds, lakes and streams; some live on the sea. They feed on insects trapped on the water, holding them with their fore legs.

Nymphs similar to adults and with similar life style, but smaller. Wing buds develop externally, enlarging with each molt until with the final molt they become wings.

Common **water striders** (illustrated) live on ponds, Pacific water striders live on the sea. The similar water measurers have very thin, elongated bodies and very long legs; they are wingless and live on vegetation or on the water of ponds. The stouter water treaders live amongst thick vegetation.

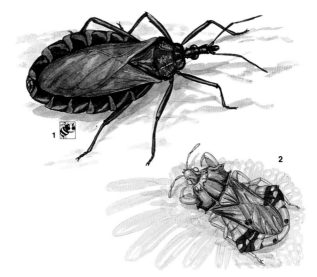

Assassin Bugs

Over 100 species. Robust or elongated, usually brown bugs, ¼–1½in long, with long legs; front legs are spiny & used for catching prey. Often the abdomen is broader than wings. Found in much of N. America. Many assassin bugs, including the thin, elongated thread-legged bugs & spined assassin bugs, hunt insects on flowers & leaves of plants. Masked Hunter hunts bed bugs & other indoor insects. **Blood-sucking Conenose (1)** sucks blood from people & may carry disease.

Ambush Bugs (2)

About 20 species. Small stout-bodied, sculptured bugs, ¼–½in long. Abdomen broader than wings. They are camouflaged in color & outline, & lie in wait on flowerheads, especially of composite flowers, for their prey. They catch other insects like bees and flies, which they seize with their grasping, thickened fore legs, & then suck them dry. Found throughout the USA.

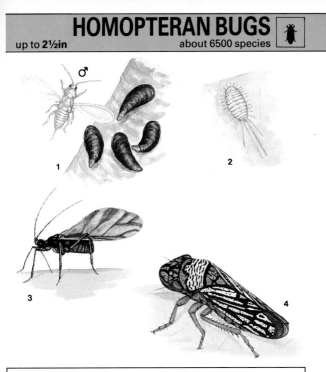

Mostly small insects with two pairs of similar membranous wings (i.e. homopterous) or wingless. Wings often held in a roof-like position over the body when at rest. All have sucking mouthparts which originate far back beneath the head.

All feed on plants, sucking out their juices with their sucking mouthparts. They may be found on any part of a plant, from roots to leaves, stems, flowers and fruits.

Nymphs similar in form to adults but wingless. Life cycle may be normal with nymphs developing through several molts into adults, or may involve alternation of winged and wingless forms, as in aphids.

Many are destructive pest species on economically important plants. They include cicadas, aphids, whiteflies, hoppers, scale insects and mealybugs. Illustrated on this page are **Oyster Shell Scale Insect** (**1**); **Longtailed Mealybug** (**2**); **Cottonwood Aphid** (**3**); and the **Sharpshooter**, a leaf hopper (**4**).

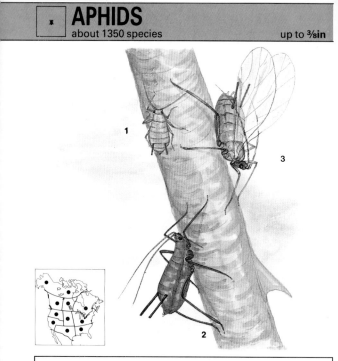

Small, soft-bodied, pear-shaped insects, usually green, brown or red, winged or wingless. Wings held vertically over body. Pair of cornicles (wax-producing organs) are present at the rear of the abdomen. Aphids have a pointed sucking "beak."

Pests of cultivated and native plants; often present in large numbers, causing leaf distortion and weakening of plants from which they suck sap. Often tended by ants for their honeydew.

Wingless females hatch from eggs in spring on host plant, and produce wingless, then winged females. These fly to different plant and multiply again. In fall winged forms fly to original plant to produce males and females. Eggs laid, then overwinter.

Aphids attack many trees like conifers, oaks, willows, maples, apples, cottonwoods, and native plants. They also attack crops like wheat, corn, legumes and cabbages. Garden pests include **Rose Aphids** (nymph (**1**), wingless form (**2**) and winged form (**3**) are illustrated) as well as lily and chrysanthemum aphids.

WHITEFLIES

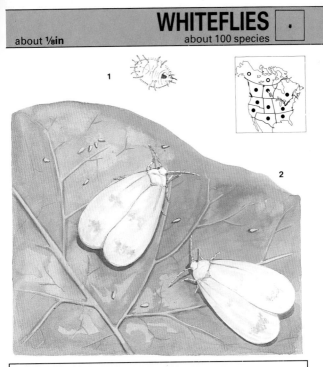

Adults tiny, covered with a white powder and with transparent, whitish or spotted wings. They look like tiny moths, with two pairs of proportionally large wings. Hind wings slightly larger than fore wings.

Mostly tropical insects. USA species live mainly on native plants in southern and southwestern states, on the undersides of the leaves. One is a greenhouse and houseplant pest.

Nymphs (1) are tiny oval creatures, attached to the undersides of the leaves by minute threads. Final nymph resembles a pupa. Nymphs and adults suck sap from leaves and cover them with a sticky honeydew on which molds grow, turning it gray.

Whiteflies are found on a large number of southern plants. Some are pests, attacking grapes, citrus, azaleas, irises and hibiscus. The **Greenhouse Whitefly** (2) lives outside in the south and also attacks a wide variety of greenhouse and house plants in the north. Nymphs resemble scale insects.

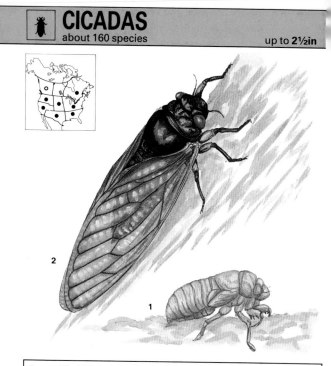

Large, blackish insects, often with green markings. They have two pairs of similar membranous wings, the fore wings twice as long as the hind wings. Males make a distinctive sound with sound boxes located at the base of the abdomen.

Males gather in groups, high up in trees and bushes to sing their songs, often just before sunset (the whole animal may vibrate), and to attract females.

Eggs laid in crevices of twigs which wilt and fall to the ground. Nymphs (1) dig into soil and suck the juices from tree roots. After a period of years, varying with species, they emerge, climb into a tree and molt to become adults.

Periodical Cicada nymphs remain underground for 13 or 17 years before they emerge to become adults (2); they all emerge together in the same year in any one place. Other cicadas have shorter life cycles, often of 3 to 4 years. One such species, the Dogday Cicada, sings on hot days in late summer.

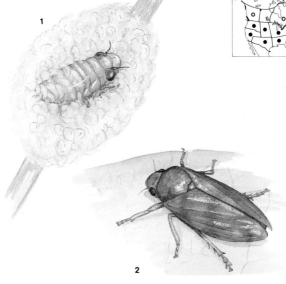

Adults jump like tiny frogs. They are oval or elongated insects, usually brown or gray in color. The pronotum is large but does not extend over the abdomen. The two tiny antennae arise on the front of the head between the eyes.

Adults and nymphs are found in meadows, gardens and woods. They suck sap from a variety of plants, especially on the new growth, and may cause considerable loss of vitality.

Nymphs are called spittlebugs (1) since they live in masses of bubbly froth which protects them from predators. They produce the froth by secreting spittle from the anus; it trickles over the body and mixes with air to make bubbles.

Most froghoppers and their nymphs live on grasses and weeds, like the Rhubarb Spittlebug which is found on docks, rhubarbs and dandelions. Some are pests, like the **Meadow Spittlebug** (2) which attacks clovers and alfalfa, in meadows and fields; others are pests on cotton, pecans and pine trees.

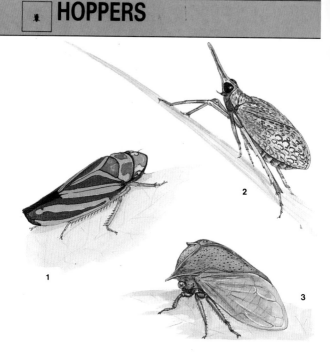

Leafhoppers

About 2500 species. Small, jumping insects like long froghoppers, up to ⅝in long, many brightly colored. The two antennae arise on the head between the eyes. Found in meadows, orchards, gardens, woods & forests throughout N. America. Many cause shriveled & discolored leaves, loss of vitality or death to plants, by sucking their juices. They may transmit fungus diseases. Many exude honeydew & are attended by ants. **Scarlet & Green Leafhopper** (**1**) feeds on native & cultivated plants.

Planthoppers

675 species. Wedge-shaped, jumping insects, with a horn on the large head. Antennae arise on sides of head beneath eyes. Suck juices of many plants. **Partridge Scolops** (**2**) lives in eastern USA.

Treehoppers

About 260 species. Very large pronotum often conceals whole body, as in **Buffalo Treehopper** (**3**), & may provide camouflage. Two antennae arise below & to the front of eyes. Commoner in south than north. Mostly live in trees & shrubs. Many exude honeydew & are tended by ants.

Large insects with long back legs and two pairs of wings. Fore wings long, narrow and leathery, protecting membranous hind wings which are folded beneath fore wings when at rest. Head flat-sided with large biting mouthparts. Pronotum large.

Found on and feed on plants, biting pieces off. Jump and glide rather than fly. Males make characteristic sounds or "songs" which they use in territorial and courtship behavior.

Most adults lay eggs in summer and fall which then overwinter and hatch in spring. Nymphs similar to adults but wingless; wing buds develop gradually, enlarging with each molt. Nymphs are found in same places and have same life style as adults.

Includes short-horned grasshoppers and locusts, many of them voracious pests which attack crops; katydids or long-horned grasshoppers; and crickets and mole crickets. Illustrated on this page are **Green Valley Grasshopper (1)**; **Jerusalem Cricket (2)**; **Snowy Tree Cricket (3)**; and **Lubber Grasshopper (4)**.

Antennae short and stout, less than half the length of head and thorax combined. Males make a low buzzing sound by rubbing rough surface of the femur of the hind leg on hardened veins on fore wings. Eardrums present on each side of abdomen.

Active by day; males "sing" loudest in hot sun. Most common in grasslands, semi-arid plains and mixed woods with the majority of species present in south.

Most short-horned grasshoppers have one brood, laying eggs in summer and overwintering as eggs but a few hibernate as adults or nymphs. Nymphs live in similar habitats to adults; they are like small adults with developing wing buds instead of wings.

Many, like the **Differential Grasshopper** (illustrated), the migratory Clearwinged Grasshopper and bird locusts are destructive pests. Others are familiar roadside and town species, like the Carolina Grasshopper and the Sulphur-winged Locust. **Lubber grasshoppers** are larger, with shortened wings.

106

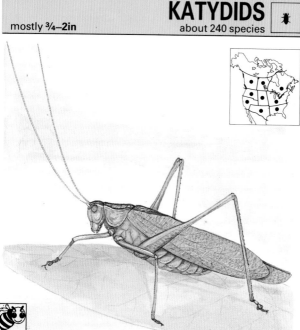

Antennae long and slender, often longer than body. Males make sound by rubbing fore wings one against the other; right wing has a rough patch which is rubbed against a vein on left. Eardrums present on fore legs. Female has sword-like ovipositor.

Nocturnal singers. Each species has a characteristic song. Adults are found in wet grassland, marshes and forest edges. They feed on tender parts of plants and on other insects.

Nymphs appear in early summer and live in similar habitats to the adults, but may remain close to the ground or live in dense vegetation. They are like small adults with developing wing buds instead of wings.

Bush katydids, like the **Forktailed Bush Katydid** (illustrated), are brown or green and live in trees and shrubs. The pale green true katydids live in similar places. The smaller meadow katydids are found in damp grassland. Mormon crickets and shield-backed katydids are brown or black.

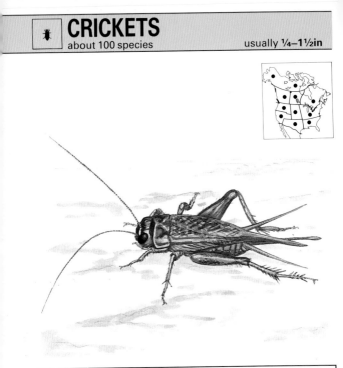

Broad, flattened insects with long antennae, up to half the length of the body. There are long conspicuous tail filaments at the end of the abdomen. Males produce sound by rubbing fore wings together. Females have long cylindrical ovipositors.

Nocturnal. Males produce a high proportion of the sound on a summer night, chirping or trilling. Adults feed on leaves, fruits and seeds but do relatively little damage.

Eggs laid in ground or in rows in plants where they may damage twigs. Nymphs are similar to adults; they appear in spring and summer and feed on plants like the adults. Wing buds develop gradually, enlarging with each molt.

The pale green **tree crickets** are found mostly on bushes and trees; many are common, singing by day or night and several may sing together. Field crickets live in grassland. **House Crickets** (illustrated), found around houses in summer, may go inside in fall and may damage woolen clothes or carpets.

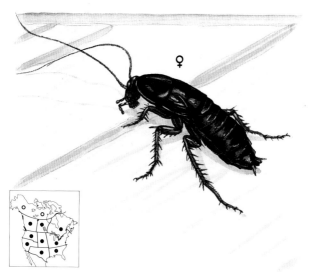

♀

Flattened, oval, reddish-brown insects. Head hidden by pronotum. Antennae long and slender. Fore wings thickened and covering the folded, membranous hind wings when they are not in use; but wings may be absent.

Many are fast-moving scavengers in houses, restaurants and stores, hiding by day to emerge by night and feed. They contaminate what they do not eat with their musty odor.

Female carries around and then lays eggs in leathery egg capsule in dark crevice. Nymphs are like miniature adults but wingless. Wing buds, if present, enlarge gradually with each molt; nymphs have similar life style to adults.

American Cockroach has large wings and flies; it is present in warm buildings throughout the continent. The cosmopolitan **Oriental Cockroach** (illustrated) is dark reddish-brown; males have shortened wings but females are wingless. Nymphs appear early in the year, often in large numbers.

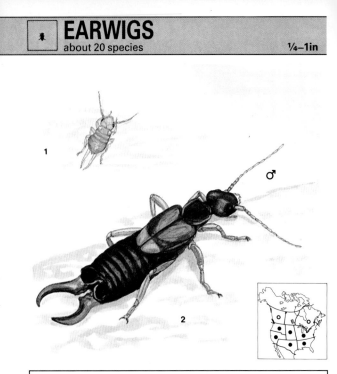

1

♂

2

Elongated, flattened, leathery, brown or black insects with characteristic forceps at end of abdomen. Antennae about half the length of the body. Some are wingless, most have short hard fore wings that cover the folded membranous hind wings.

Live in damp places, crevices, under bark or in soil. They are omnivorous. Some are pests in flower gardens.

Nymphs (1) similar to adults, but often paler and softer and with wing buds that enlarge with each molt. Many live in family groups until they become adults, guarded by mother, in similar places to the adults.

Common earwigs are the most familiar and include the introduced **European Earwigs** (2), which are garden pests that feed on flowers. Red-legged Earwig is a wingless form that is found in debris in southern USA. Longhorned Earwigs live near water and possess very long forceps.

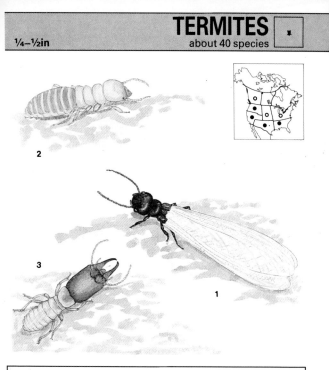

Pale, soft-bodied, cylindrical insects with no waist between thorax and abdomen. Workers and soldiers are wingless, fertile males and females have two pairs of long membranous wings (1) when they swarm but soon lose them. Wings have no cross veins.

Males and females swarm often in sunshine after rain. They pair off, lose their wings and each pair digs a burrow and forms a new colony. They bore into and feed on wood.

Termites live in large colonies with a caste system of fertile king and queen, workers (2) and soldiers (3), plus nymphs. They do not leave the nest, except to swarm; workers do not forage, for the colony lives in the wood which is their food.

Subterranean termites (illustrated) nest in soil, making extensive galleries and earth shelters; they feed on wood and can be destructive to houses if there is contact between soil and wood. Powder-post termites attack sound wood of houses, poles and trees. Desert termites live in soil of southwest.

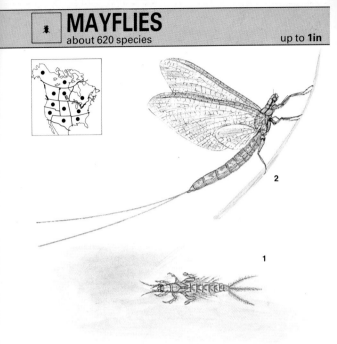

Insects with soft brownish or yellowish bodies and two or three long tail filaments. Most have two pairs of wings. Fore wings large, rather triangular in shape with many veins and cross veins and fluted margins; smaller hind wings similar.

Nymphs emerge from water to become immature adults, molting to become adults within 48 hours. These live for a few days or less. Males gather in swarms, often several feet above ground.

Nymphs (1) live in lakes and rivers, in bottom mud, under stones, in moss or crevices on the banks. Up to an inch long, they have abdominal gills and three long tail filaments. They emerge in summer from the water to become adults.

Common burrowing Mayflies, like the **Golden Mayfly** (2), grow up to an inch long. Spinners and small mayflies are smaller (up to a half inch long). All are found near slow moving rivers or ponds where the nymphs live. Stream mayflies live near streams where their nymphs hide under stones in flowing water.

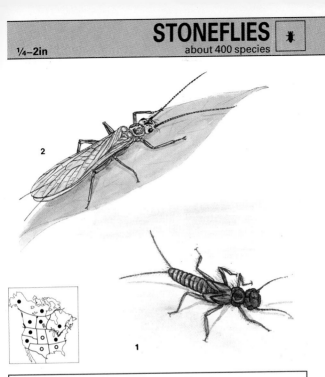

Large soft-bodied, flattened insects with two long antennae on head and two long tail filaments on abdomen. The two pairs of large membranous wings have many veins. When at rest the broader hind wings are folded with fore wings over abdomen.

Stoneflies are most common in northern and mountain areas. Adults are poor fliers and are most often found under stones, on tree trunks or resting on vegetation near water.

Nymphs (1), like smaller wingless adults, have filamentous or tufted gills on thorax and abdomen. They live under stones or debris, usually in streams with unpolluted, well oxygenated, clean water. They have two long abdominal tail filaments.

Common stoneflies are widespread in summer and most likely to be found on vegetation near streams. Giant stoneflies emerge in summer and may be attracted to lights. **Predatory stoneflies (2)**, are seen in late spring and early summer, near water. Winter stoneflies fly in winter and spring.

113

DRAGONFLIES
about 280 species   1–3½in; wingspan ¾–5½in

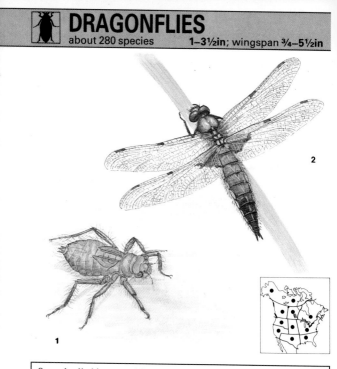

Stout-bodied insects with two pairs of large membranous wings. Wings have complex veins and cross veins. When at rest they hold their wings horizontally to the sides. The head is large and freely movable with large eyes and biting mouthparts.

These are large predaceous insects which pursue their prey, other insects like mosquitoes, on the wing. They fly over and near water, often patrolling low along a definite route.

The large nymphs (1) live in water of ponds and streams, feeding on other water insects, catching them with a "mask," a large hinged lower lip which can be swung out at lightning speed to grasp the prey.

Skimmers, like the **Four-spot Skimmer** (2), are large brilliant dragonflies seen flying horizontally across shallow water or resting on plants. Darners, also large and brilliant in color, may be seen far from water. Clubtails are medium-sized dragonflies with a club-shaped abdomen, often found along streams.

1–2in; wingspan ¾–3in   about 120 species

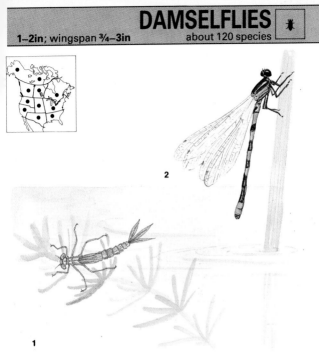

2

1

Smaller relatives of dragonflies. They have slender bodies and two pairs of large membranous wings with complex veins and cross veins. When at rest they hold their wings together over their back. They have large heads and eyes like dragonflies.

Adults live near water. They spend much of their time resting on vegetation, darting out at passing prey like mosquitoes or midges, and fly much more readily in sun than in dull weather.

Nymphs (**1**) live in water of ponds and streams, like dragonfly nymphs but can easily be distinguished from them by the three plate-like gills at the tail end of the abdomen. They catch their prey with a mask in the same way as dragonfly nymphs.

Broad-winged damselflies, like blackwings and rubyspots, are large damselflies with broad wings and black or green slender bodies; Narrow-winged damselflies have wings that are stalked at the base and slender bodies; they include the dancers and the bluets, like the **Circumpolar Bluet** illustrated (**2**).

115

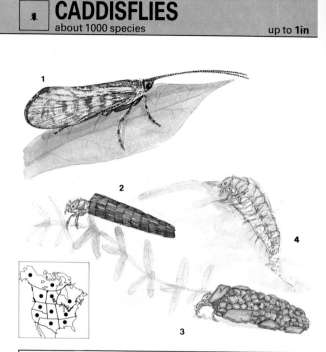

Elongated, cylindrical, soft-bodied insects, brown or yellow in color with no tail filaments. They have two pairs of large, membranous, rather hairy wings which are held in a roof-like position when at rest. Antennae as long as body or longer.

Nocturnal. Adults (**1**) are poor fliers with erratic flight but may be attracted to lights at night. Hide by day in crevices or vegetation near water and feed but little.

Larvae are like caterpillars, with three legs on the thorax, two hook-like prolegs on the abdomen. They live in water, many in cases of wood pieces, sand grains or shell fragments; others spin nets or live in cocoons or mud tubes.

Casemaker caddis larvae make cases out of plant fragments like the **Giant Casemaker** (**2**), sand grains, or stones, like the **Northern Casemaker** (**3**); they live in ponds and streams. **Free-living caddis** larvae (**4**) live in parchment-like cocoons in fast-flowing streams, clinging to rocks.

116

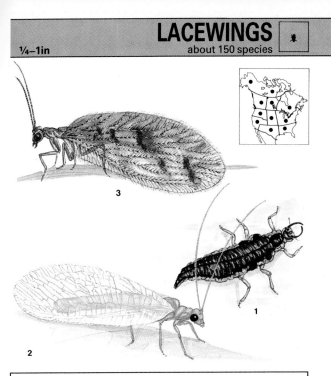

3

1

2

Soft-bodied, green or brown insects with two pairs of membranous wings, usually held in a roof-like position over the body. Wings have many net-like veins. Antennae long. Lacewings have no tail filaments.

Green lacewings are found in grassland, gardens and other open areas. Brown lacewings live in woods and forests. They all feed on aphids, scale insects, mealybugs and mites.

Green lacewings lay eggs under leaves, each suspended by a long slender stalk; larvae (1) are flattened and elongated. Brown lacewing eggs are not stalked; their larvae are similar to those of green lacewings. All feed on pests like adults.

There are about 90 species of **green lacewings** (2); they are the larger (½–1in) of the lacewings and are green with green wings and golden eyes. There are about 50 species of **brown lacewings** (3). They are smaller (¼–½in) and are brown with brown wings and brown eyes.

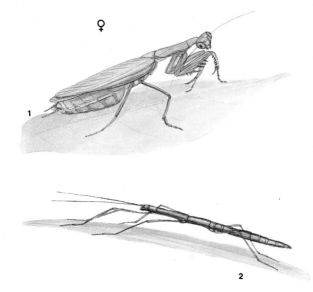

♀

1

2

Mantises

20 species. Elongated insects with cylindrical, leathery bodies & long, slender antennae. Usually green or green & brown. Hind wings membranous, fore wings thickened & cover hind wings when at rest. Front legs very large & modified for catching prey, with spines along inside edge for holding prey. Found on trees & shrubs, sitting motionless or stalking prey. Some are attracted to lights at night. **European Mantis (1)** is introduced & now common in many parts of the USA.

Walkingsticks

About 30 species. Elongated, leathery or hard insects with long legs, green or brown in color. They may either be cylindrical or flattened & leaflike. Antennae long. All but one Florida species are wingless. Walkingsticks live in trees & shrubs, hiding by day & imitating leaves or green twigs, & feeding by night. They may be kept as pets. **Common Walkingstick (2)** lives on oak, black locust & wild cherry.

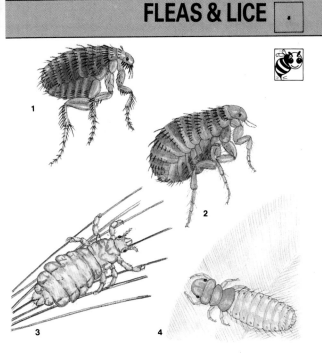

Fleas
325 species. Brown or black, wingless insects, flattened from side to side, up to ¼in long. Most have hard bodies with many spines & bristles. Hind legs are long & used in jumping. Fleas live in nests & lairs of birds & mammals. They include **Cat Fleas** (1) and **Human Fleas** (2). They suck the blood of their hosts, piercing the skin with their sucking mouthparts. They may carry diseases like typhus & plague. Eggs are laid in debris or dust & the larvae feed on hairs & other organic remains.

Sucking Lice
56 species. Wingless, oval or circular, pale, flat-bodied insects, up to ¼in long. Legs are short & bent inwards, adapted for clinging to hair. Parasites, living on mammals & sucking blood. **Human Head Louse** (3) lives on the head.

Chewing Lice
About 950 species. Elongated or oval, bristly, wingless insects, up to ¼in long. Clinging legs small & stout. Parasites living on mammals & birds, feeding on feathers, hair, skin or blood. **Hen Louse** (4) lives on hens & ducks.

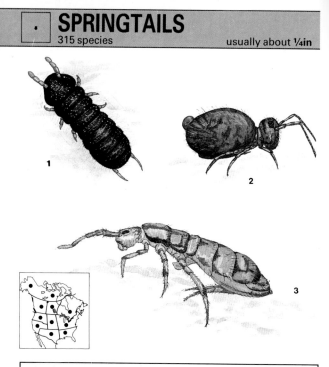

Tiny, soft-bodied, wingless, usually elongated insects. They vary in color, most are white or gray, others are yellow or brown. A tube protrudes from the first abdominal segment and a two-pronged "tail" is bent under the end of the abdomen.

Springtails can spring suddenly into the air if the flexion of the "tail" is suddenly released. They are found almost everywhere but are most common in soil, plant debris and on water.

Nymphs are just like smaller adults in outward appearance, and they are found with them in similar places.

Water Springtails (1) live on the surfaces of ponds, lakes and streams. Seashore Springtails live in crevices of seashore rocks. **Globular Springtails (2)** live in leaf litter, mosses, in rotting wood, in soil and in caves. **Slender Springtails (3)** live in similar habitats and may be pests in greenhouses.

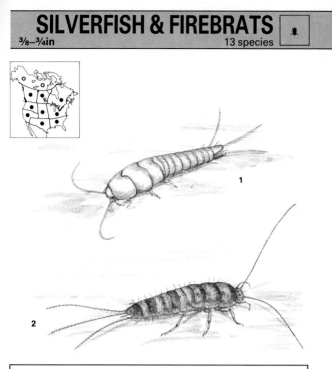

Soft, flattened, wingless insects, brown or silver-gray in color and covered in scales. They have three long tail filaments on the abdomen and two long antennae on the head. Eyes are small and wide apart.

Found in houses; these insects run quickly into hiding if disturbed. Silverfish feed on dried starchy foods, book bindings and paper glue. Firebrats eat kitchen scraps.

Nymphs are similar to adults and have a similar life-style. They take about two years to mature.

Silverfish (1) are covered with tiny silvery scales; they live in closets, behind bathtubs and bookcases. **Firebrats** (2) are brown and gray; they live in warm places, near furnaces and heating pipes. The related bristletails live in soil, leaf litter, rotting wood and caves; also on the seashore.

INDEX

All species in Roman type are illustrated

Ants	76, 89	Golden Buprestid	22
Carpenter	76	Green June	31
Apanteles	83	Ground	18
Aphids	100	*Ham*	26
Cottonwood	99	Hercules	14, 30
		Hide	29
Backswimmers	98	Japanese	31
Bee Killers	64	*June*	30
Bees	76	Ladybird	34
Bumble	80	Larder	29
Carpenter	76	Leaf	32, 33
Hive	81	Longhorn	15
Honey	81	May	30
Leaf-cutting	79	Metallic Wood-boring	22
Mason	79	Milkweed	15
Mining	78	*Minute*	14
Resin	79	Oil	21
Sweat	78	Predaceous Diving	36
Beetles	14	Rove	20
Ambrosia	27	Sap	39
Antlike Flower	38	Scarab	30, 31
Asparagus	32	Sexton	39
Bark	27	Shining Flower	38
Blister	21	Soft-winged Flower	38
Bombardier	18	Soldier	25
Carpet	29	Spotted Cucumber	32
Carrion	39	Stag	17
Case-bearing	33	Tiger	16
Checkered	26	*Tobacco*	28
Click	23	Tortoise	33
Clown	14	Tumbling Flower	38
Colorado Potato	32	Water	36, 37
Crawling Water	37	Water Scavenger	36
Darkling	19	Whirligig	37
Death Watch	28	*Blackwings*	115
Dried Fruit	39	Blood-sucking Conenose	98
Drugstore	28	Bluebottle	71
Dung	31	Bluets	115
Eleodes	19	Borers, European Corn	54
Flat Bark	14	Flat-headed	22
Flea	33	Great Pine	15
Flower	31, 38	Peach Tree	55
Furniture	28	Round-headed	15

Bugs	90	Wood Nymphs	47
Ambush	98		
Aquatic	96, 97	Caddisflies	116
Assassin	98	Cicadas	102
Bed	90	*Clubtails*	114
Cactus	93	Cockroaches	109
Chinch	94	Crickets	105, 108
False Chinch	94	Jerusalem	105
Harlequin Cabbage	95	*Mole*	105
Lace	92	*Mormon*	107
Leaf	91	Snowy Tree	105
Leaf-footed	93		
Milkweed	94	Damselflies	115
Negro	90	*Dancers*	115
Plant	91	*Darners*	114
Predatory	98	Dragonflies	114
Seed	95		
Squash	93	Earwigs	110
Stilt	90	Eyed Elator	23
Stink	95	*Eye Gnats*	75
Thread-legged	98		
Buffalo bugs	29	*Fairyflies*	85
Buffalo Gnats	63	Firebrat	121
Butterflies	40	Fireflies	24
Admirals	45	Fleas	119
Anglewings	45	Flies	57
Arctics	47	Bee	66
Blues	43	Black	63
Brush-footed	44	Blow	71
Checkerspots	45	*Bulb*	67
Checkered White	40	Crane	60
Cloudywings	46	Dance	57
Coppers	43	Deer	69
Crescents	45	Drone	67
Duskywings	46	Dung	57
Fritillaries	45	Flesh	73
Gossamer Wings	44	Frit	75
Hackberry	40	Fruit	72
Hairstreaks	43	*Hessian*	61
Milkweed	47	Horse	69
Orangetips	42	House	70
Monarch	47	Hover	67
Mourning Cloak	44	Long-legged	74
Prairie Ringlet	47	March	57
Queen	47	Moth	74
Question Mark	45	Parasitic	68
Satyrs	47	Peacock	72
Skippers	46	Pomace	72
Sootywings	46	Robber	64
Sulphurs	42	*Screw-worm*	71
Swallowtails	41	Seaweed	75
Tortoiseshells	44	Shore	75
Viceroy	44, 47	Snipe	57
Whites	41	Soldier	65

Stable	70
Trichogramma	85
Winter Crane	60
Froghoppers	103
Galls	61, 84
Glow-worms	24
Grasshoppers	105
Green Valley	105
Long-horned	105
Lubber	105, 106
Short-horned	106
Homopteran Bugs	99
Hoppers	103, 104
Hornets	86
Hornworms	52
Ichneumons	82
Katydids	105, 107
Lacewings	117
Leafhoppers	104
Lice	119
Locusts	106
Maggots, Apple	72
Rat-tailed	67
Root and Seed	73
Mantises	118
Mayflies	112
Mealworm	19
Mealybugs	99
Midges	59
Biting	62
Gall	61
Mosquitoes	58
Moths	40
Alfalfa Looper	40
Armyworm	50
Calif. Spanworm	48
Cecropia	53
Clearwing	55
Clothes	55
Codling	54
Dagger	51
Dart	51
Eight-spot Forester	50
Fall Cankerworm	48
Gelechid	55
Giant Silkworm	53
Gypsy	56
Hawk	52
Inchworm	48
Io	53
Lichen	49
Luna	40, 53
Orange Tortrix	54
Owlet	50
Pinion and Sallow	51
Plume	55
Potato Tuberworm	55
Prominent	56
Snout	54
Sod Webworm	54
Sphinx	52
Spruce Budworm	54
Tent Caterpillar	56
Tiger	49
Tortricid	54
Tussock	56
Underwing	51
Wasp	49
No-see-ums	62
Partridge Scolops	104
Pennsylvania Leatherwing	25
Planthoppers	104
Punkies	62
Rubyspots	115
Sawflies	77
Scale Insects	99
Sharpshooter	99
Silverfish	121
Skimmers	114
Snail Eaters	18
Spanish Fly	21
Spittlebugs	103
Springtails	120
Stoneflies	113
Tarantula Hawks	88
Termites	111
Toe-biters	90, 96
Treehoppers	104
Tumblebugs	31
Turkey Gnats	63
Walkingsticks	118
Wasps	76
Aphid	83
Braconid	83
Chalcid	85
Cuckoo	88

Digger 87
Gall 84
Horntail 76
Mud Daubers 76, 87
Paper 86
Sand 87
Spider 88
Thread-waisted 87
Yellowjackets 86
Water Boatmen 96
Water Measurers 97
Water Striders 97
Weevils 35
Bean 14
Whiteflies 101
Wireworms 23
False 19